OF
CABBAGES
&
KINGS

By Jacob D. Eppinga

ZONDERVAN
PUBLISHING HOUSE   OF THE ZONDERVAN CORPORATION
GRAND RAPIDS, MICHIGAN 49506

The majority of this material was previously published in the column "Of Cabbages and Kings" by Jacob D. Eppinga in THE BANNER, official organ of the Christian Reformed Church, 2850 Kalamazoo Ave., SE, Grand Rapids, Mich., and is used by permission.

OF CABBAGES AND KINGS

Printed in the United States of America

CONTENTS

"The time has come," the Walrus said,
   "To talk of many things:
Of shoes—and ships—and sealing-wax—
   Of cabbages—and kings—"

   —from *Through the Looking-Glass and
   What Alice Found There,* by Lewis Carroll

,?¢!

Dear friends,

Once upon a time there was a man called ",?¢!." Unlike many of his generation whose names were meaningless, his was most descriptive of himself—just like those names in Bible times.

,—This meant that he was young and that by the measure of threescore years and ten, his life was far from over, as a period(.) might indicate.

?—This meant that he had an inquiring mind and asked questions about a lot of things.

¢—This meant that he was neither rich nor poor, but that his needs were met by the modest wages he earned.

!—This was the best part of his name by far. It indicated that he was a Christian who shared Paul's exclamation: "The Son of God, who loved me and gave himself for me!" (Gal. 2:20).

Because Mr. ,?¢! had accepted Christ, he wished to join a church. First he went to an Irish Catholic church, but he didn't feel at home. Father O'Malley and Father O'Houlihan surely tried to make him welcome. In fact, they proposed to place an O' in front of his name too. That would really make him one of them. But ,?¢! wanted to be accepted as he was, and so he left.

Next he went to a Greek Orthodox church. He was

welcomed there too. In fact, Bishops Christianoupolis and Charioupolis wanted to baptize him ,?¢!polis immediately. But ,?¢! liked his name the way it was.

Then he went to a Scandinavian Lutheran church. Pastors Emilson and Helgerson were friendly and jolly. "We'll make a good Lutheran out of you," they said. "We'll just stick a 'son' at the end of your name and who will know the difference?" But by this time, ,?¢! was getting a little bit discouraged.

So he went to a Dutch Christian Reformed church. Again he received a hearty welcome, though more serious and less jolly. The consistory held a meeting on his request for membership and immediately faced a serious problem. Seeing as how ,?¢! was so different and wasn't even in the alphabet, where would they list him in the membership book? The problem was solved by placing a "van" in front of his name and an "a" behind it—Van,?¢!a.

This made "," (short for ,?¢!) very sad.

"The others were bad enough," he said. "They wanted to change my name either at the front or at the back. But these Christian Reformers want to make me over at both ends.

"Can't anybody just take me the way I am?" he cried.

P.S. *Jesus did.*

ADAM BLAMED EVE

Though I am "American born," I had never heard of a Colorado beetle until I arrived in England. It is true, of course, that I am no authority on the subject of insects. It is also a fact that my mind is far from encyclopedic. Still, having lived in the United States of America all my life, having had my share of science and biology courses in high school and college, and having traveled through a slice of Colorado a few years ago, you might expect that I would have run across a Colorado beetle at least once—if not in the flesh, then certainly in a book. That is, if such a creature, in fact, existed.

You can readily understand my reaction, therefore, when this Englishman, a farmer in Cambridgeshire, had the gall, in my presence, to blame his potato failure on this imagined creature from the United States.

"Dash it all," I said to him, using one of his own typical expressions, "I object! I rise to the defense of my country and its Centennial state. If beetles destroyed your old spuds, they were probably English! Her Majesty's subjects and all that sort of thing! Why must you people, and all other countries for that matter, always blame America for your troubles? It's utter balderdash," I added, again throwing in one of his typical expressions.

My ire was certainly not diminished when later that same day I picked up the evening edition of the *London Times* and read a medical report on the alarming increase of French pox in the United Kingdom. Well, at least they were not accusing us of that! But why blame France? Syphilis, as sin, surely has no nationality. It's no more rife in the shadows of the Eiffel Tower than it is in the environs of Big Ben! Another piece of chicanery!

"At least in America," I thought, "we don't put the blame for our problems and troubles on the other fellow."

But I was wrong.

Coming home, I spied in our backyard a gadget by the bushes. Some government man forgot to collect it last fall. It's a device for trapping beetles. What kind? Japanese beetles! But why call them that? I saw one once, and it didn't look the least bit oriental. Nor did it bear a "made in Japan" label. It appears, then, that I owe an Englishman somewhere in Cambridgeshire an apology. We are no better than our British cousins. In fact, we may be *worse*. I haven't the time to research this matter completely, but it seems to me quite a few of our ills and troubles are blamed on others.

German measles, just to name something. I had them once upon a time, and, as I recall, they were as American as apple pie. All the other kids on my block had them too—among them Italians and Polish and Belgians. As a matter of fact, the one kid on our street who couldn't catch them, though he tried hard enough, was Donald. And he was Lutheran, which in those days meant that he must be German, just like if you were Christian Reformed you must be Dutch. But if he didn't have them, then why blame Germany for those blotches on your skin, like we blame the Japanese for those blotches on our leaves?

Or what about Asian flu? I never heard of American flu in this country, though I am sure, just like every-

12

thing else, we don't take a back seat to anybody, even in the bug department. We can build them bigger and "badder" than anybody, and probably do. So why blame Hong Kong or those millions of Asiatics when we call the boss and tell him we won't be in today?

To mention just one more item, there is that Dutch elm disease. We lost two elm trees because of this affliction, which is just a small part of the tens of thousands more, all over our landscape, that have succumbed. We hope we can lick this problem. Meanwhile, as long as it is with us, we put the blame on the noble land of my ancestors! Disgusting.

But let me take this pen out of my cheek. If the above is a little wacky, at least the point is good. Trouble is always identified as somebody else's product. We learn it from Adam (Gen. 3:12). Disorder and disturbance in your church or mine is never your fault or mine. We always label it with somebody else's name.

ALL THE LONELY PEOPLE

"Many hand kisses," said the postcard from Amsterdam. "In hour I fly Budapest." T.N.

Twenty-five years ago T.N. was a lawyer in Hungary and a government official. But when the machinery of World War II ground to a halt, he was marked. For some political sin, never defined, the Communists banished him to Siberia. When he returned a decade later, he had aged twenty years. A broken man, he was, nevertheless, grateful to be back in his own dear country. But ten months later the ill-fated revolution broke out in the streets of Budapest, causing him to stumble to Austria, where, together with some other refugees, he was gathered in by the American government and flown to New York for asylum.

A church in Grand Rapids, Michigan, sponsored him. He arrived at the Union Depot, where a committee of strangers, speaking a strange language he never learned to master, met him. They provided food, clothing, and a place to live. And work. He tried some janitorial duties. He polished brass in a downtown bank. But he really couldn't manage the simple tasks and assignments. Too much had been squeezed out of him. In Siberia. And the church committee understood.

There were a few trips to the hospital. In the summertime there was a garden to grow hot peppers in and a Grand River to sit beside and throw a baited line in. And a few friends. But the friends, though kind, were mostly busy friends, for America was a busy land.

The streets grew dangerous. He was assaulted and robbed by punks looking for easy prey. He was moved to a better location—an apartment. But apartments have no gardens. And moved again to a hotel where his meals could be provided. And then, because of amnesty, it became possible for him to return to his beloved Budapest again. His friends arranged it. He could see a few remaining relatives and talk with one and all. No language barrier anymore. Home for Christmas! With European courtliness and quiet dignity, he bade his few friends good-by. He took the plane to Amsterdam, sent a card on which he scratched with his uncertain hand, and boarded the plane for home—a man who had not had a home for a quarter of a century.

A cable was received from the State Department: "T.N., who arrived in Budapest December 2, 1970 from Grand Rapids, Michigan, died of a pulmonary embolism December 26."

☼   ☼   ☼

They called him Jeremiah—all five feet of him and barely ninety pounds. He wore a maxi or, rather, a secondhand coat meant for someone twice his size and weight and a Texas hat that engulfed his tiny face. Oh, but his eyes! They seemed strong enough not only to look through buildings, but even people. That's why they called him Jeremiah—for those eyes and for that sequoia of a cane he never was without.

He lived in a third-floor room in a fourth-rate hotel, blazingly hot in summer, but always neat. He remembered being married long ago, and he remembered a minister in the old country who had been defrocked for something so terrible he never could bring himself to tell. That's why he would sometimes stand up in the front row, in the middle of my sermon, with that gaze.

He had two prize possessions: a large theological tome written in his native tongue, so heavy with fine print that he could not lift it, and a zither that he played but could never hear, no more than the sermons in the church, for his ears were as dull as his eyes were sharp.

Jeremiah no longer walks the streets of our town. Nobody noticed much when he was gone. For in a busy world we seldom note the prophets, or those who look like them. He went to a pauper's grave; his zither went to the Salvation Army store, where, for a time, it hung silently in the window. When I spied it there, I thought I saw his eyes again. Then it, too, disappeared.

✿ ✿ ✿

Sometimes a congregation adopts a person. With Mr. P. it was the other way around. He came from the country with above three-score years on his back and less than a dozen in his mentality. The first in church each Sunday, he prizes the bulletins he cannot read and shakes hands with as many as will extend their own. A child in his seventies, with rheumy eyes and a roomier heart, he knows what church is all about. "He died for us," he said one Easter day as he shook my hand for the fifth time that morning. It was a Good Friday remark on Resurrection Sunday, yet, therefore, no less to the point.

In his room he has a picture—his favorite—of the Mackinac Bridge that straddles the straits between Upper and Lower Michigan. "It's way up north," he says, as he stands in awe of me for having seen it. I must take him there someday, though right now I am too busy. Meanwhile, between Sundays, Mr. P. takes his lonely walks, waiting for winter to turn to spring.

✿ ✿ ✿

He was rejected of men (Isa. 53:3).

Could you not watch with me one hour (Matt. 26:40)?

16

My God, why hast thou forsaken me (Matt. 27:46)?

*   *   *

All the lonely people. . . .
Where do they all come from!
   One came from Hungary.
   Another came from the Netherlands.
   A third came from "the country."
   And one came from heaven above, not too busy to
     save us from the loneliness of sin.

AN OLD STORY IN MODERN (UN)DRESS
(With apologies to Hans Christian Anderson)

The Old Story

Once upon a time there were some rogues who posed as weavers. They promised the emperor, who was always fond of new clothes, that they would make him a most wonderful garment. It would contain colors and patterns more realistic than he had ever seen before. Furthermore, they continued, the materials would have the unusual property of being visible only to the sophisticates, remaining invisible to all who were unfit or extraordinarily simple in character. The emperor agreed and so, rogues that they were, they proceeded to pretend to weave.

After a while the emperor sent his faithful old minister to preview the work of the weavers in order that he might have a progress report. But the faithful old minister saw nothing whatsoever. Only empty looms. Believing the falsehood disseminated by the rogues that only the worthy could see the materials, he was greatly shaken in his self-confidence. Was he, in truth, a simpleton? He could see nothing at all, no matter how much he strained his sight. But not wishing his wisdom and worthiness to be questioned, and unwilling to risk his job, he reported to the emperor that the garment, in process, was indeed exciting to the eye.

The emperor sent others to inspect as well. They,

too, saw nothing whatsoever. Yet they, too, not wanting to be considered unfit, reported that the garment in the making was both supercolossal and terrific. Finally, the emperor went himself. Seeing nothing, he was greatly discomfited. Apparently he alone was unworthy and simple, for all sang the praises of what eluded him. Unwilling to reveal himself as a simpleton, however, he, too, praised the work of the rogues.

When the pretended garment was completed, the pretending weavers pretended to dress the emperor for the premiere parade down the broad way so that all the citizens could see. But all they saw was their emperor in the nude. Wishing, like everyone else, to appear knowledgeable and wise, all shouted their praises of the beautiful technicolors and patterns of the emperor's new clothes. All, that is, except some children. They could see nothing but an old man with no clothes walking down the broad way. Being unsophisticated and innocent, they simply told their elders that all they saw was a naked man.

In Modern (un) Dress

Once upon a time, in the recent past, there were some rogues who posed as moviemakers. They promised the people, who were always fond of films, that they would produce some new and most wonderful creations: celluloids clothed with patterns of such significance and socially redeeming qualities as had never before been seen. Furthermore, they said that those who would not be able to see anything in their productions would thereby reveal themselves as being clods and squares. Only the socially aware and progressive would be able to discern and see. And so, rogues that they were, they proceeded to pretend to weave their great cinematic finery.

After a while the people sent a faithful critic to preview the work of the moviemakers in order that they might read a review. But the faithful critic saw nothing at all of what was being trumpeted as both significant and socially redeeming. However, believing the falsehood disseminated by the rogues that only the sophisticates and progressives would understand and see and, furthermore, not relishing the risk of being labeled a clod and a square and such similar titles which could only succeed in losing him his job, he reported to the people that the cinematic efforts he had seen were, indeed, exciting to the eye. And soul.

The people sent other critics, but they, too, saw nothing whatsoever. Yet not wanting to be considered uncultured and dull, they reported in the entertainment pages of the newspapers that what they saw was both supercolossal and terrific. All of this, of course, heightened the expectancy of the people who could not wait to see the great productions which were clothed with significance and dressed in socially redeeming qualities.

The day of showing arrived and the great premiere took place on the broad way where all the citizens could see. But none saw the apparel of significance, and none saw the dress of socially redeeming qualities in which the celluloids were supposedly arrayed. All for the simple reason that they were not there. What the people did see was dressed only in underwear—and even less. Afraid to speak the truth, however, thus running the risk of being considered unsophisticated, all shouted their praises of the beautiful cinematic significances and technicolored socially redeeming qualities. Even some churches and church publications joined in praises, for they, too, did not wish to be considered unprogressive. Only the children took exception. Being unsophisticated and innocent, they said that all they saw was a bunch of naked people.

ANTIANTIDISESTABLISHMENTARIANISM

Someone has said that the Roman Catholic church is the most orthodox, conservative, traditionalist, and authoritarian establishment in the Western world, but torn presently on a dozen different fronts. It might have been added that some Protestant churches, too, are affected by the ferment of this century. With the passing of the years, many denominations are changing. This is alarming to some. This is encouraging to some. To still others, it is a little bit of both.

The fact is that we have varied reactions to the present state of our church, its vitality or lassitude, and the directions it must take. Our convictions here do not always coincide. These differences are sometimes not the result of doctrinal disagreement so much as they are a result of variations in our psychological make-ups.

We are not peas in a pod. We are a fellowship of progressives, conservatives, traditionalists, innovators, and the like. Within the circle of Christian commitment, a whole spectrum can be found.

I think God planned us this way. And how wonderful! Surely it would be dreadful if all God's children were identical! It is in this connection that I think of "the biggest word you ever heard," which is not supercaliphragilisticexpialidocious, as the song says— for that is not a word. But rather, antiantidisestablish-

21

mentarianism—which is a word, and which is as rich in meaning as it is in letters, of which there are some thirty-two. Breaking it down and building it up again, we have establishment-disestablishment. In this sequence, there can be found not only the pendulum of history, but also the pendulum of our church, without whose swing our clock would stop.

Some of us are establishmentarians. To the core! We want to keep things the way they are. Better yet, we would like to go back to the way things were. At any rate, we are in favor of deepening the stakes (Isa. 54:2). Establishmentarians tend to be older in years, but not necessarily, and tend to grow more establishmentarian as the years go by, but again not necessarily.

Some of us, on the other hand, are disestablishmentarians. We always talk about adjusting to the age so that we may be relevant as a church. Our emphasis is on "widening the tent" (again Isa. 54:2) in order to touch life on all sides. Disestablishmentarians want change, fresh ideas, new approaches. Less patient, they want to meet the needs of these times of great transition!

We owe a large debt to the establishmentarians. They have kept us close to the fundamentals of our faith. The church owes a great debt, likewise, to the disestablishmentarians. Without them, our denomination, for example, would still be holding all its services in Dutch. God grant, then, that we may always have both types within our fellowship. Or, better yet, the best of both spirits within each member. Both sides desperately need each other. Where there is only establishmentarianism, there is eventual stagnation. Where there is only disestablishmentarianism, there is eventual revolution. But where both can exist, in tension, there renewal will be found in continuum.

But what about antidisestablishmentarianism? And antianti-? It is here that the word changes meaning in my dictionary. The more elongated it becomes, the more acrimony it contains, the less the Spirit of God it has. For whereas establishmentarians and disestablishmentarians fight for ideas, the antidisestablishmentarians and the antiantis fight against people. The first pair of words is positive and legitimate; the second is negative and destructive. The antidisestablishmentarian is the fellow who fights "liberals"—not actually, but so labeled, while the antianti snorts and looks down his nose at those who are hopelessly behind the times.

Speaking of our denomination, an earnest young Christian said recently, "If we play our cards right (Old Maid, of course), we will hold on to the fundamentals of the faith, while at the same time 'making the scene' in each new decade." But for this to happen, it is required that both the "stake deepeners" and the "tent wideners" work together.

APATHY

A nationally syndicated columnist recently laid a charge at my church door—and yours. It was the allegation that, though society reels, so many of us are apathetic. Is he right?

There is evidence that he is, and that we are, in large measure, a fellowship of the unconcerned. Not, of course, about ourselves. This is good—but only up to a point. Beyond that point lies the realm of spiritual hypochondria, a world wherein we become so preoccupied with self that there is no time for others.

The church lives largely in that world. No wonder, then, that there rises out of her bosom one son who writes a book entitled *The Comfortable Pew,* another named Pike who had a pique, and more like him—individuals whose views may be heretical but whose concerns are often right. And how ironic that sometimes those of us in Zion who decry their appearances are unaware that it is our own ease in Zion that has produced and created them.

Soren Kierkegaard, the Danish philosopher, told a story. There were some geese, he said, who could talk. Every Sunday they met for worship. One of the ganders would arise and preach about their lofty destiny as geese, for with wings provided by the Creator they could fly high, wide, and free. And all the geese nodded happily in agreement with such sermons and came back every week to hear more. Meanwhile, during the week they ate and grew fat, visited and drank coffee, and talked about some of their outstanding ancestors who, in their day, flew high! However, none of them tried to fly, having a fear of heights. Occasionally one would attempt the feat and fall, sustaining an injury here or there. When that happened, the others would raise their eyebrows as if to say, "Who does he think he is?" Said Kierkegaard: How many of us are like those geese, agreeing with sermons we hear on flying, but then waddling home, growing fat, and never trying our wings?

Without presuming to improve on the Dane, what if Rev. Gander had also preached on the sorry story of geese in general: of how the majority of them were going to the dogs, inundated by wars, race problems, crime, alcoholism, addiction, immorality, rotting cities, and all the things that make for stress and hate and misery. As a matter of fact, I presume he did. I further presume that these messages, too, left the feathered congregations moved, yet not enough to act.

If Jesus in heaven, before He came to earth, had harbored the apathy that is ours, would He ever have come to Bethlehem? Sometimes I think I hear the church singing a paraphrase of one of the songs from *My Fair Lady:* "The Lord above gave the church an arm of iron, so it could do its work and never shirk. But, with a little bit of luck, someone else will do the work!" I was angry when I read what the columnist laid at my door—and yours. But there is too much truth in his allegation for me to have the right to bristle.

So, let me lay my apathy aside. Christianity is a religion of verbs, not nouns. Even its greatest proper noun, "Jesus," when all is said and done, is a verb. It means, "He will save his people from their sins" (Matt. 1:21).

John Wesley understood this verb—"religion." He traveled 250,000 miles on horseback, averaging 20 miles a day for 40 years, preaching 40,000 sermons. At age 83, he was annoyed that he could not write more than 15 hours a day without hurting his eyes. At age 86, he was ashamed that he could not preach more than twice a day. And he complained in his diary that there was a growing tendency in him to lie in bed until 5:30 in the morning. And . . . .

But excuse me. I am getting out of this chair. I am going to work. Coming along?

26

ASSURANCE OF FAITH

It was a discussion about hell! How we hit on the topic in a mixed group, and in a relatively untheological setting, belongs to the mysteries of those rambling conversations whose twistings and turnings are impossible to trace. Asserting its reality, I was immediately asked, being the only preacher in the crowd, to present the group with a description of the place—a request which, never having been there, I could not easily fulfill. I said it was the complete absence of God, even as heaven is His complete presence. I added more such remarks as were, in my view, theologically sound and biblical. But I could tell I was losing some of my listeners—especially the younger ones. What they wanted from me, I gathered, was something less theological and more dramatic, in the style of a Milton or a Dante or a Jonathan Edwards. Not being in a class with these giants of the past, however, I could not oblige. The best I could do was to recall a conversation with one of my sons a number of years ago.

It was a beautiful summer evening in the north country. We were camping in a lovely place hard by Lake Michigan, and the fishing that day had been very good. But every silver lining has a cloud. So, too, a stringer full of fish. Catch them, and you must clean them. Son number one, a fisherman from birth, had been carrying his weight in this department admirably, whereas son number two, no fisherman at all, had avoided this drudgery on the grounds that he should not be made to clean what others had caught. Because his appetite for fish exceeded everyone's, however, I decreed on this night that he should assist his father and thus initiate himself into the mysteries of the scaling, decapitation, and evisceration of marine life. Accordingly, he accompanied his father into the gathering dusk, with his allotment in a pail.

Now the evening was hot and sticky. The mosquitoes were thick as flies and the flies as stinging as mosquitoes. The advantage was all theirs, for with hands wet and "fishy," defense was difficult. Son number two, however, labored on with little complaint, though I could tell that his desperation equaled mine. When he did speak, it was to startle me with—of all things—a theological question.

"Dad," he said, "what do you think hell is like?"

Now I must confess that matters theological were, at that particular moment, farthest from my mind. I warned him, therefore, that he ran the risk of getting a foolish answer by way of asking a foolish question. But he ignored my observation, answering his own question.

"I think hell is like cleaning fish forever and ever, with insects biting you forever and ever, so that you can't slap your neck and face forever and ever."

It was an interesting observation. Not in the style of a John Calvin, perhaps, though certainly in the tradition of Dante's *Inferno*. I found myself winding along a similar mental path. What did I detest most of all? Automobiles? No. I disliked them second worst. What I hated most of all was monthly bank statements and trying to make my checking account balance.

So, without being in the least facetious, I answered my young son and said, "I think hell is like getting a monthly bank statement every day forever and ever,

28

and never having your account balance forever and ever, yet always having to try—forever and forever."

Having recalled this incident for the entertainment, if not benefit, of my listeners, I felt myself on top of the situation. I was now in a position to direct their own question away from me and back at them. "What do you think hell is like?" I asked, turning in the direction of my host, my Dutch cousin. Up to this point he had not participated in the conversation, though he had listened well. An imaginative sort, and with a sense of humor, all expected a semi-serious reply from him.

"What do I think hell is like?" he repeated. "To tell the truth, I have never thought about it."

"Why not?" I pressed.

"Why should I bother about it?" he said, and then added the punch line: "I'm never going there anyway."

It was humbly stated, for my Dutch cousin is a dedicated Christian. And the more I thought about it, the more I liked what he said. It was a simple statement of faith and rich in that assurance that may be the possession of everyone who belongs to God and who takes Him at his word. "Him that cometh to me, I will in no wise cast out." There are more such expressions in the Holy Scriptures.

What is hell like? If you are not a Christian, you do well to read Christ's description of it: "There shall be weeping and wailing and gnashing of teeth." But if you are a Christian, by God's grace—why bother with the question? Whatever it's like, you're not going there.

AWARDS

Leafing through a church supply catalog the other day, I came upon a few illustrated pages of medals and awards which Sunday schools can purchase and ceremoniously bestow upon their brighter and more faithful little Christian warriors. The sight of these badges, to be worn on small lapels or dresses, brought back distressing memories for me.

I remembered a rather obnoxious Sunday school colleague of mine, age eleven or so, who regularly flaunted his "pin" in my face. My chest region was bare while his was conspicuously bemedaled. Not only did he have a nice blue-and-gold badge with the words "Sunday school" written on it, but in addition there was attached, beneath the badge, a small bar with letters on it saying "first year," and attached to that another one reading "second year," and still another under that saying "third year." Imagine that! Three years of perfect attendance—and all that hardware to prove it! It was like he was a general in the army of God and I wasn't even a private.

The real reason he was so decorated was not because he was so godly, but because he was so healthy. And the real reason I was so undecorated was not because I was so ungodly, but because I suffered periodically and painfully with earaches. I recall a cold or two, as well, and a fever which I tried to hide from my parents so that I wouldn't be forced to stay home from church and thus spoil a perfect attendance record I was working on. Yes, and I remember an all-important Christmas program in which I had to bear the frankincense, which I missed, having been felled by yellow jaundice.

It is true, of course, that I too had my little victories and accomplishments of which I could boast. My piano teacher had pasted several gold stars in my "School for the Pianoforte" book, Volume I, by Theodore Presser. But that was hardly the kind of thing you bragged about to your friends, unless you wanted to be labeled a sissy. The sum of the matter was that I ended up, in self-defense, disliking Sunday school.

Since those days of my childhood we have made great advances, presumably, in the field of child psychology. Why, then, do some of us still hand out "perfect attendance" awards?

BACK TO GOD?

I

The man spoke with great feeling. He was talking about the state of the church, and he was also pushing his finger into my stomach. I don't like it one bit when people push their fingers into my stomach.

"I think our denominational radio effort should be given a different label," he was saying. "*Back to God Hour?* What kind of a name is that? It's a bad title, and there's everything wrong with it. The biggest problem, of course, is that it ignores one of the simple and basic rules of all human psychology which tells us to avoid negative concepts when we are on the selling end of things. What we need is a radio name with a forward, not backward, flow to it." He removed his finger for a moment to reinforce his last statement with a gesture.

I listened, retreated a step on sighting his returning finger, and nodded some agreement. I couldn't think of anything that went counter to his reasoning. That was one big trouble with me. I couldn't marshal arguments quickly. It did bother me a little that he showed so much feeling on the subject. Frankly, I couldn't get that worked up about it. The fact is that I had never really thought much about our denominational radio label.

"Speaking about psychology," he continued, "I believe there are other words and phrases in the vocabulary of the church that show a similar feature to accentuate the positive. Take that word 'retreat.' We have adult retreats, young people's retreats, weekend retreats, et cetera. Why don't our churches get smart and schedule congregational 'advances'?"

I couldn't think of anything against this idea either. Frankly, all that came to mind was a joke. I considered warning him against getting the ladies of the church together for some advances. But it was a bad joke. Anyway, he wouldn't get the point, and I was still getting his finger.

"Same thing with a lot of sermon titles I see in the paper. No good," he said. "Take last week's church page with all those ads. One preacher was speaking on *The Failure of Man*. Now there's a negative title if ever I heard one. Another announced *The Speck-Tacklers* as his subject. Nothing big about that. Still another had *Faith Walks on Fallen Arches* as his theme. That's flatter than feet can ever get. How do you expect to attract with titles like that! What you fellows have to do is eliminate the negative. *The Positive Possibilities of Probability Thinking.* There! I just made it up. It's an example of what I'm after. *Back to God?* Take that title out of reverse and throw it into forward gear if you want to go, go, go."

Up against the wall by this time, I was wishing he would throw his finger into reverse. I also wished he would take a church for a while. I'd like to see how well he could do. Come to think of it, though, he had more of a point than just his finger. Eluding his final prod, I said good-by to him.

Walking down the street, I tried to get myself all psyched up with his psychology. Forward march. Push, push, push.

"*Onward Hour*"—that would be a good name for our radio program! I would write to the committee and make the suggestion. What a sluggish bunch to be satisfied with that old title so full of retrogression! First, though, I ought to do something about the name of my own church. Get some life into it. I mean—how would we ever get anywhere ignoring one of the simple and basic rules of all human psychology which tells us to avoid negative concepts when we are on the selling end of things?

My church's name is LaGrave—taken from the street on which it is located.

How sepulchral can you get!

11

The next morning was Sunday. I had slept fitfully, as I always do when facing some extras in the service. There were several babies to baptize, and I hoped I would concentrate hard enough to get their names correctly. It happens, sometimes, that I can read one word but say another. I think this is a sign that I am not completely normal. I remember baptizing someone David when the card in my hand plainly said Daniel. I knew it was wrong when I said it.

Mistakes are one thing. Deliberate mistakes another. But errors that are both voluntary and involuntary simultaneously don't make any sense at all.

Besides the baptism, some young people were going to make profession of faith. This, too, had to be done correctly. It was an added concern, subtracting even more from my sleep.

Everything went well with the baptisms. I said all the babies' names correctly. But my performance sagged a bit during the profession of faith. I had read the formulary and was addressing the questions to those fine young people standing before me. I had finished the first and had started on the second.

That's when it happened! My eyes settled on the coming words. I was about to ask them if they "abhorred themselves."

Suddenly I felt that finger in my stomach again. There wasn't anything wrong with the question. I was going to ask them if they abhorred and humbled them-

34

selves before God because of their sins. Surely Paul had done this, too. Even so, there has always been something about self-abhorrence articulated in a profession of faith that makes it more a profession of sin than of faith. Certainly on this occasion the emphasis should be on the happiness and joy of being new creatures in Christ!

So there I was, reading the words while at the same time processing all these other thoughts. And at the same time thinking how odd and abnormal it was to be doing both things at once.

But I couldn't help it. Back to God Hour. Retreats. The failure of man. The speck-tacklers. LaGrave. Abhor yourself. And everybody knows that one of the simple and basic rules of human psychology tells us to avoid negative concepts when we are on the selling end of things. These and more thoughts kept flashing through my mind as I continued reading the question. By this time, I was also holding a protective hand over my stomach, as if expecting my friend with the finger to materialize. I finished and was ready to ask for answers.

"Don," I said, "what is your reply?"

There! I had done it again.

His name was Ron.

III

The week following was a blinger. I always laugh when people make jokes about how easy preachers have it. Why not? I know that most of them are kidding. But just in case somebody hasn't heard it yet, let me say that the hours involved in the ministry aren't exactly what the labor unions have in mind.

It wasn't my schedule, however, that made the week unusual. Instead, it was a telephone call, followed by a letter. A church in the East had held a congregational meeting and had voted to invite me to become its pastor. Strange what such a development can do to a person's power of concentration!

How do ministers arrive at decisions regarding the calls they receive anyway? I remember hearing their letters of reply read in the services when I was a boy. Our pulpit had been vacant for ever so long as preacher after preacher declined our invitation. It was not God's will that they come. So they wrote. But how did they know? I wondered about that. Did God send them postcards from heaven telling them "yes" or "no"? Or were their decisions based purely on human factors? I listened once when a man my mother didn't like came over to talk to my father about something. She didn't like him, she said, because he was irreverent. My father asked him if he thought the latest minister we had called would come. The man said it depended on the minister's wife. Then he told a story about a preacher's daughter who was asked whether her father was going to accept the call which he had received from another church.

"Well," she said, "father is in the study praying, but mother is in the bedroom packing, so I'm sure he'll go."

That story bothered me for a long time.

I remember some years ago when I received a string of calls. Some came from churches that didn't know me from Adam, whatever that means. Every time I turned one down, my wife wanted me to finish washing the walls in the living room. But then another call would come just in time to save me from that chore. After all, I might accept—in which case, I wondered why I should bother to bathe walls for my successor. And so they didn't get washed for a long time.

In those days there was an old seminary professor who, in my opinion, was a real man of God. I drove five hours one day to talk to him about how I should determine the Lord's will about church calls. As I might have expected, he couldn't say exactly. Still, he helped me just a bit.

"When you receive a call," he said, "take the letter and lay it on your bed. Then get down on your knees and show your letter to the Lord. Tell Him that you are going to weigh this matter seriously because you want to do His will. Then enter into a kind of agreement with Him. Say that in three weeks you are going to make a decision, one way or another, and that in that period He should direct all your thinking and everything that happens to you in such a way that you will be influenced in the right direction. Tell Him that while He is doing all His directing and influencing, you are going to be practical in your approach and will make your final judgment based on all considerations.

"After this," said the professor, "get up from your knees and place your plan, proposed to God, into action. He'll live up to the terms you laid down for Him if you will honor those you laid down for yourself. Nine chances out of ten, it will end up coming out His way."

As I said, he was helpful. I tried to practice what he preached. Gradually, though, I developed an additional technique. Not just for considering calls, but for facing anything really crucial in my life.

"Are you fixing to turn the clock back again?" It was my wife who asked the question. But it was rhetorical.

I had to—in order to decide that call.

IV

My father was a great lover of animals. Despite the fact that we lived in the middle of a congested metropolitan area and despite the fact that our place was something less than ample by some standards, we shared our lot with rabbits, pheasants, chickens, homing pigeons, turtledoves, tropical fish, canaries, guinea pigs, and more.

It was my father's contention that there was much to be learned from watching all these animals. He pointed out that I should consider how certain species cared for their young. He said that as every sluggard

37

could go to the ants for a lesson, so many an indifferent parent could profit by watching a mother hen.

With these lessons, among others, drilled into me, it was small wonder that years later I pulled off the road to watch a man with a horse. He was leading the animal a small distance to a fence. Reaching it, he made the beast retrace his steps, walking backward. Then he led it at a trot to the fence again.

When this performance had been repeated a number of times, my curiosity overcame my reticence. I asked the reason for this odd procedure. The man said he was a trainer, and the horse was having its first lesson in learning to jump obstacles. This was the way it was done.

"Ahm learnen 'im somethen, mister. A hoss has to know 'e can't jump unless 'e fust backs off."

I didn't make the application immediately. In fact, for years I remembered that trainer—not for what he said, but for how he said it. It became a line I quoted, and for no reason, at odd and idle moments. Driving my car. Taking a walk. Finally one day the truth penetrated my dull skull.

"It's the same with people," I thought.

Something else again—learned from the animal world. A running broad jump beats a standing one all hollow. And as for the standing high jump—it doesn't exist. A man must retreat in order to advance over a hurdle. Sometimes he must back up in order to go ahead. *A man has to know 'e can't jump unless 'e fust backs off.*

It was this to which my wife referred when she asked if I was about to turn back the clock. It was another of those abnormal things I did. On occasion, facing great decisions, I felt the need of revisiting the scenes of my childhood. It helped me gain perspective. The Danish philosopher Soren Kierkegaard once said that although life must be lived forwards, it can only be understood backwards. Poking about the old neighborhoods, I found this to be true. Looking back helped me to see ahead. Hindsight gained foresight. Turning the clock of my life in reverse was a form of backing up by which I gathered momentum to surmount whatever call, crisis, or hurdle had temporarily interrupted my gait.

Not everything I know, such as it is, has come from books and professors. Indeed, one valuable lesson I learned came from neither. If it didn't come to me straight from the horse's mouth, at least it came to me from his trainer!

V

It was a beautiful day. I had left my house early in the morning because I wanted to spend as much time as possible in my hometown. Should I accept the invitation received from that church out east? What was God's will? Did I really expect to find the answer on the street where I grew up?

My first stop had to be at the old doughnut shop. There had been a time when I never passed it without entering. Doughnuts, spelled "donuts," were made on the spot right before your eyes—the best in all the world. Though the place wasn't what it used to be, looking slightly down at the heels, the same sign still greeted every customer:

> As you go through life, brother,
> Whatever be your goal,
> Keep your eye upon the donut,
> And not upon the hole.

I remembered how I had been criticized in my seminary days when, in some church somewhere, I had quoted those lines in a sermon. Afterwards, the leading elder took me aside to tell me that poems about donuts had no place in the Christian pulpit. He said I should have looked around in the Book of Proverbs where I could find that same sort of stuff, only in more dignified language.

I remember how his remark bothered me when I went to preach that same fledgling sermon in another little church. I had grown immensely fond of that verse as a youngster. I remember when it was first explained to me. Focus on the donut, and it will seem large and the hole small. Stare at the hole, and it will loom larger than what surrounds it. That's what my father had said, and it was true.

I thought about my friend with the finger. I'm sure he would like those words up there on the wall. They fitted in well with that simple and basic rule of human psychology which tells us to avoid negative concepts, like holes in donuts, when we're on the selling end of things. Like Pavlov's dog, I put a protective hand over my stomach as I ordered one plain and one glazed and a cup of coffee.

I was glad I had come. It was true that the homely homily on the wall didn't exactly decide my call for me, but it did set things in perspective. I had been feeling a bit burdened by that call to serve another church. It meant a big decision, and I didn't like decisions. What a system we had! Far better to have a bishop who would move preachers around. Particularly, if I could be that bishop.

But the sign shifted my mental gears. It reminded me that there was a bright side at which I should be looking. Better to be burdened by decisions to make than never to have any to make at all. From this point, my mind went on and on. There was something of God's everlasting "Yea" in that rhyme staring at me that made it significantly Christian in my eyes—a long-forgotten elder notwithstanding. Were there holes in donuts in Paradise? But now that the holes are here, though Paradise is not, the Lord wants us to put the emphasis on the positives, and not the negatives, in life.

By this time I was imagining myself in the pulpit. Do what you can about the holes of sin! Indeed, take them seriously! Meanwhile, rejoice! And again I say, rejoice in that which surrounds the hole in creation, and is much bigger, namely—your salvation!

I would probably never preach such a sermon. It was too corny.

Two more donuts later, one chocolate, one sugar, I rose to leave, feeling very round and satisfied with myself.

VI

Henry Ford said that history was bunk. Obviously I disagreed with him as I drove his product into my own history, searching for the street where I grew up. It was my belief that looking at what lay behind might help bring into focus something of what lay ahead.

But how narrow the streets were and how close together the houses stood! Nostalgia set in, yet anger, too, as I looked at the old homestead. I remembered moving into it when it was spanking new, built by my father. It had seemed a palace. Now its dull windows were like sad staring eyes, no recognition dawning in them at the sight of me. The neighborhood dwellings looked equally unkempt. Someone came out of the side door from which I had emerged, youthfully, a thousand times on my way to school. She eyed me with suspicion as I stood lonely on the walk. I thought of the words: "He came unto his own and his own received him not." The text didn't really fit, but it came to mind anyway.

Why do our cities have to rot, and why must the old neighborhoods deteriorate? I remembered looking at my father's birthplace, and my grandfather's, back in the Netherlands. Those houses, though infinitely older, are still standing clean and vigorous and full of life, vital units in warm neighborhoods. By contrast, the site of my youth now spoke to me of decay and danger.

I recalled a graduation day years before when we had heard Eddy Guest, poet laureate of our fair city. How wonderfully true, we had all agreed, his words had been to parents and their sons and daughters. "It takes a heap o' livin' in a house t' make it home." But now I stood a stranger here—less changed myself than my old dwelling place, and wondering what kind of a heap of something on the part of all society it takes to make a home a house.

I had come to ask myself a question. Loitering in my own past, I had wanted to look at my own small footprints in the sidewalk to inquire what God's further purpose was for the lad who had surreptitiously put them there. Instead, I was off on a tangent as I looked at a part of me standing there begging for a coat of paint.

I was thinking of a teacher of theology. I had been his student. In the classroom he was always taking us back to Paradise. It was his contention that there were no theological or philosophical solutions to any problems apart from a consideration of man's beginnings. In a time wherein men were discarding Genesis, he was asserting its supreme relevance. What is the chief end of man? What are the purposes of God? What is everything all about? What is the meaning of life? What is the order of all things? What is the nature of evil? It was Paradise that held solutions to them all. Indeed, whatever answers ignored the Garden of Eden were bound to be wrong answers.

All this, he steadfastly insisted, was supremely true of the greatest question in all the world, namely—Who is Christ? Here, especially, we were urged, to go back to man's lost garden for the definition—the Second Adam.

Suddenly I thought of my friend again—the one who made points on my stomach, if not my mind. He would probably not approve of my standing there, backed up three decades into my past. I looked around, half expecting to see him—finger and all. Why hadn't I thought to answer him with my old teacher's point of view! What an affliction—not being able to marshal arguments readily.

So here I was, back in my boyhood paradise. Time had evicted me. Meanwhile, no angels had stood with flaming swords to keep it all untouched, unspoiled. Instead, blight and weeds and sagging foundations were cursing the ground and successfully challenging man's dominion.

I was starting to homilize again. When I came out of my reverie, I noticed that I was wet. Nature had come abustling, as if belatedly attempting to freshen things with soft rain for my reception. But I was as ready to go as I was unready for what was ahead.

VII

I made my way deeper into the inner city. I wanted to see the school I had attended as a boy, a squat, square, two-story affair of dark red brick. I wanted to walk around it, touch it, and wander again across the tiny playground which, when I was a youngster, had always impressed me as so ample. I had done this before on a few occasions when, facing other decisions, I had found the old place helpful in discovering my bearings.

It had been a parochial school, owned and operated by a denomination other than my own. Indeed, some of its classes had even been conducted in a foreign tongue which it had been necessary to learn. But such had been the convictions of my parents that they preferred Christian teachers in another language to uncommitted ones in familiar English. Some of their friends had disapproved of their policy as heartily as they had pitied me as its victim. Dear Mrs. Pratt and Mrs. Simpson, wonderful neighbors and very English, could not understand why I was made to go miles on a streetcar every morning to a German school.

The fact was that I had loved it. Some of my happiest experiences had been at St. Paul's. That's why it had been so hard, the last time, to see the building empty and abandoned. What had been even worse was the three police officers who had stopped for an explanation of my presence. They had warned me against lingering, saying it wasn't safe.

Even so, I wanted to stop by again, if for no other reason than to hear the laughter of the playground in my memory and to imagine the stern face of Mr. Seitz lining us up and marching us into the adjoining church for morning prayers. There was something about that old building that I couldn't put into words. It made me more real to myself. I would stand there again and say, "Here is where I learned to read and think. Here God started my formal education. What did He have in mind with me?" I would try to relate such backward glances to my future plans.

But I was in for surprise and shock. Rounding the final corner, I discovered that this Rock of Gibralter of my life was no longer there. It had been removed. What had become more than a landmark in my life simply no longer existed. I felt like astronauts returning from the moon only to discover that in their absence the earth had disappeared.

"And the place thereof shall know it no more," I thought. This time the text was really appropriate, but I couldn't quote it as offhandedly as people sometimes do when commenting on man's changing scene. People go into buildings. But buildings also go into people—something that unfeeling wrecking balls and bulldozers do not understand. What some past generation had sacrificed for and dedicated to God had been rendered rubble and expendable by time, change, and more. Two children approached and passed.

"What's he doing?" asked one.

"He's lookin' at nothin'," said the other. But that wasn't true. The fact was that I was seeing a lot while beginning to understand a little the unutterable sadness of people—like Albert Camus who wished Christianity was true—but it wasn't; who wished there was a God—but He didn't exist.

I thought of a wistful friend and understood his sadness a little better than I had before. Reared in the Christian faith, secure in his beliefs, he had come to manhood and to the belief that God did not exist. I had prevailed upon him once to attend a service. Afterwards, he had said that he would not come again, for the experience was too painful. He said that it was like going back to something wonderful, only to discover it wasn't there. The hymns had made him cry, and the prayers had but increased his loneliness. He said it had been like a visit to a beautiful cemetery, talking to one who couldn't hear. Even worse—an empty tomb, yet empty not because of a resurrection. For what could live again that had never lived at all?

In a clearing in the inner city and looking at nothing, as a small pedestrian had observed, I discovered God anew. Back to God? How unutterably devastating to the soul to go back to Him only to find that He isn't there. Yet, this is not the truth of the thing. He is always there—unmoved. Whoever goes back to Him in any age finds Him in any age. The wrecking balls of unbelief and the bulldozers of a thousand philosophies cannot touch the Rock of Ages. Because of who He is and what He is, going back to Him is never like going back to an empty field. Indeed, those who go back with open eyes and open hearts will gloriously discover that He not only is, is, is, but as the writer to the Hebrews adds, "is a rewarder of those who diligently seek him."

There! I was homilizing again.
Only this time it wasn't corny.
It was good!

VIII

I was home again. I had traveled in search of an answer to a question. Instead, I came back with a message for a friend. This time it was my finger that would do the walking on his chest and stomach. I flexed it for the duel. It would not be easy. He wore double-breasted suits.

I found him soon enough. Never dull, always interesting, yet never having learned that it was impolite to point, he followed his finger across the room in my direction and in the manner of one who knew all about one of the simple and basic rules of all human psychology which tells us to avoid negative concepts when we are on the selling end of things. Yet, this time, I was too fast for him.

Even so, I almost flubbed my opening. He wanted to know why I called him Harry when his name was Larry. I responded by telling him that I really appreciated the fact that he was the kind of guy who kept his eye upon the donut.

That really did it. He was so nonplused that his finger went limp. At the same moment mine went straight to the mark, softening him up, as I talked to him about retreats. I thought I would start with those, reserving my remarks on his criticisms of our radio title for later. I told him that "a hoss has to know 'e can't jump unless 'e fust backs off." Sometimes we have to retreat before we can advance. I told him to look at some of the Psalms and also some of those speeches in the Book of Acts, reviewing God's dealings with His people. That was like backing up to go ahead, I said. And, anyway, had he never heard of Kierkegaard, who was a lot smarter than we both were, and who said that although life must be lived forwards, it can only be understood backwards?

"Ouch," he said, rubbing his stomach as he stepped backwards and I stepped forwards.

I went for one of his ribs with my finger. It made me think of Adam, so I told him about Paradise. Asking him what he was made for and what everything was all about, I defied him to answer me in terms exclusive of what was past. I said every question a man can ask

46

has to be taken all the way back to Eden for an answer, and if he thought that was a negative direction in which to go, what in all the world was more positive than Paradise!

"You're making your point," he said, holding his side. Then, eying my finger, he asked why I felt it necessary to be so emphatic. My response was another jab as I opened up the matter with which he had begun our earlier conversation. I told him that *Back to God* was an absolutely beautiful title. It implied that we had a God to go back to and who was always there. What if He wasn't? Then we couldn't! But He is! And so we can! And how is the church or the country or any man ever going to go ahead unless the church and the country and every man first goes back to Him?

I told him about an empty field in an inner city. It had contained a school and surrounding houses. But the whole neighborhood had gone bad, I said, and so the city fathers leveled everything in order to start from scratch—right from the ground on up.

Maybe, I said, that's what a lot of people have to do on the inside—start from scratch—right from God on up.

He was up against the wall. He was holding my tired finger, having captured it in self-defense. He was smiling and agreeing, and he was mumbling.

"Touché," he said.

It was satisfying to hear. I walked away in the manner of one who knew one of the simple and basic rules of all psychology which tells us to embrace positive concepts—like *"Back to God"*—when on the selling end of things.

As I was about to leave the room, Harry, or was it Larry, followed me out the door. Protecting his stomach with both hands, he asked me a final question.

"I hear you have a call," he said. "What are you going to do?"

"BANG! YOU'RE DEAD!"

Yesterday, the sight of a long lost book, *Tom Brown's School Days,* presented to me at age eleven, brought back an irresistible tide of memories. As I pored over its pages in those days, my own life seemed tame by comparison. Daily piano practice, going to catechism—what kind of boyhood was that! In retrospect, however, it seems that my young years were considerably more bloodthirsty than bland. If I must give an accounting one day for boyhood hours, I will have to admit to having given an astonishing amount of time to the perpetration of mayhem and violence.

Whole summers were devoted to playing Cowboys and Indians. Clarence Schoenborn and I owned cowboy suits. That meant that the rest of the kids had to be the Indians. We tied them to trees, imprisoned them, and shot them down in cold blood with our cap guns. I always insisted on being Tom Mix, a Hollywood star of Westerns whom I had never seen, not being permitted to go to picture shows. When we didn't play Cowboys and Indians, we played Cops and Robbers. The latter were usually labeled members of the Purple Gang (an underworld organization ravaging the city of Detroit at the time) and had machine guns that went "eh eh eh eh eh." What joy it was to go skulking between houses in pursuit of these bad guys, surprising them with ominous index fingers extended and shouting, "Bang! You're dead!"

Sundays brought a temporary truce, at least for me, for on this day of rest I was not permitted to go out and play. If anything, however, Lord's Days were even more violent, rather than less, for I had a whole army of little tin soldiers to play with in my bedroom. On my haunches (wearing a hole in the knee of the knickers of your Sunday suit brought some real violence), I lined up whole divisions and regiments, facing each other in combat. What a wonderful game it was! Sometimes when the minister would say at the end of the morning service, "Go in peace," my mind was already planning how to outflank the enemy on my bedroom floor. And, when father would make his first call to get ready for church in the afternoon, where the minister would greet us with the words, "Grace to you and peace . . . ," there was always time to polish off a whole platoon with my toy cannon and spitballs.

If you conclude from all this that such a boy as described above could only be headed for a life of violence and crime, you are obviously wrong, unless you consider my being a Christian Reformed minister a bad thing. The fact of the matter is that I was extremely sensitive to the sight of blood. The first time I saw my father murder a chicken for Sunday dinner, I couldn't eat it. And when I saw Mr. Snodgrass on the corner carried out of his Cleaners and Dyers shop, dead from a bomb because he wouldn't pay protection money, I was more sober than an alcoholic on the wagon.

All of which brings me to a point. We all subscribe to the idea that violence is unchristian and that the sixth commandment is as important as the seventh, and all the rest. In our individual and congregational prayers, we offer up fervent pleas for peace. The seventh beatitude (blessed are the peacemakers) receives our wholehearted endorsement, while "Shalom" (peace) is a word not strange to our tongues, though few of us speak Hebrew. There are even churches that have drawn up protests to the toy industry, objecting to all the war games, tanks, and bombers that are so plentiful and available for Santa's bag at Christmas time.

Yet all the while, many of us subtly go the way of a small boy of years ago, but for "real" and not "pretend." How many of history's pages have been bloodied by direct action by the church! Today, Protestants and Roman Catholics in Ireland put down their prayer books to take up pistols containing more than caps. While as for us, it is a question whether we are more involved with spreading the dynamite of God (1 Cor. 1:24—Bang! You're alive!) than the other kind.

I read in the paper that ten denominations, representing about one-fourth of U.S. church membership, have a total of nearly $203,000,000 invested in twenty-nine companies that last year produced more than $10,000,000,000 in war matériel. Add to this our many individual investments in companies producing war goods—some of the profits of which land in our offering plates—and one begins to wonder how much right we have to go to church and pray, "Thy kingdom come, Thy will be done, on earth as it is in heaven."

"We now have a wonderful new bomb," some Christian told me last week. "Nothing like the atomic one, you understand, but capable of killing everything alive in one square mile."

It's all a very complicated business, I know. But isn't it about time the evangelical churches were a little more vocal on these matters, including our own, before—"Bang! We're all dead?" We, too, I think, on the day of accounting will have to admit to having given an astonishing amount of money and consent to the perpetration of mayhem and violence in the earth.

BEHIND THE SEENS

I remember the day I lost an argument to a class-mate—one in which I had contended with vehemence that the word "library" did not contain an "r" after the letter "b." The teacher to whom we both appealed said that I was wrong.

So, too, there came a day when I first saw the expression "behind the scenes" on paper. Oddly, I had always assumed the word was "seens." It was another mistake to correct in the long process of learning. Yet unaccountably, it is an error my mind has retained through the years. Invariably, whenever someone invites me to look behind the scenes of something, my brain substitutes the wrong word, as in the title of this article, for the right one. I am not altogether unhappy with this mental quirk, however, for sometimes it adds a fresh dimension.

The purpose, then, of what follows is not to take you behind the scenes of the church, but to look behind the seens in the church. There is a difference. What my congregation sees when I appear in the pulpit always frightens me a little. I wear a robe and try to deport myself in such ways and manners as are fitting and appropriate. I read and pray and preach sermons in which my voice goes up and down the scale, sometimes in rather authoritarian ways, I suppose.

It is quite possible, therefore, that some in the congregation whose exposure to the preacher may be minimal could get the wrong impression. I remember one of my own children, very young at the time, believing that the man in the front of the church we were visiting, who was wearing a long black nightie, was God. Such cases of mistaken identity may be rare. Nevertheless, there are those who exalt the preacher, by reason of his dress and setting, to a position in the vertical ladder which he neither wishes nor deserves. Such people ought to look behind the seens.

I have a book of ecclesiastical cartoons, one of which depicts a minister in his pulpit properly attired. From the front, his appearance is one of dignity. But the rear view drawing shows his clerical gown open at the back, revealing an old pair of trousers, baggy at the knees, and the stem of a pipe protruding from a hip pocket. And so if he looks somewhat impressive from the front, he appears singularly human from the rear. In fact, if from the congregation's point of view he appears to have himself and his subject well in hand, from the vantage point of the choir he looks like a frightened individual, almost ludicrously inadequate.

It is a good cartoon for ministers to study, designed to keep them humble as well as to prevent them from taking themselves too seriously. But it is also good for laymen to ponder. It reminds them of the fact that their preachers are like unto them in all things, sin included.

Ministers, seeing their congregations before them, are more apt to be aware of what lies behind the facades and fronts that they behold. This is because, as pastors and counselors, they have been taken behind the seens by some of the individual members. They know that certain smiling exteriors hide breaking hearts, and that some proper ones conceal unholy lives. Some angel faces harbor gossiping tongues, and some worldly looking ones, by puritan standards, belong to religiously intense and devout souls. Some spiritual lives are at low ebb, despite postures seemingly intent, while others, perhaps, pigeonholed as something less than vital in the faith, would interrupt the sermon with an "Amen" if they dared.

To use a cliche, "Things are not always as they seem."

Putting it all together, there are at least two observations that must emerge. For one thing, fellow members of the congregation ought to be considerably less judgmental in their opinions of one another. It may well be that the frozen face across the aisle conceals an aching heart, and that the apparently inattentive one in the pew ahead is wrestling with some great decision, just then, in the house of God. More than once someone has said to me, "I would not have said what I did about Mrs. Blank if I had known. . . ."

The second conclusion is a glorious one. Our Lord, who goes behind the seens of all of us, including the rear view of his poor undershepherd in the pulpit, rejects none of us. He beholds all our hearts and the secrets within. Nevertheless, He loves us, one and all, as Christians, for the sake of His dear Son who presents us faultless before His throne (Jude 24).

BUMPER STICKERS

Automobiles must have horns. It is the law. But drivers may not lean on their horns unnecessarily. This, too, is the law. To blow or not to blow, that is the question.

It was this question that put me in a quandary a few weeks ago while waiting for a traffic light. A bumper sticker on the car ahead caught my eye. It said, "Honk if you love Jesus."

Years ago I read a good article by the late Dr. H. Hoeksema entitled "Hawking Religion." He was against that sort of thing. But what about honking it?

It has always been my policy to use my horn sparingly. There is simply too much noise pollution around for me to contribute to it without cause. Drivers in some other countries are of a different persuasion. I remember a hair-raising ride in Cuba years ago. Approaching small villages, the whole car seemed to lean forward, along with driver, as he accelerated down main streets. In keeping with the custom, he blew his horn all the way, scattering dogs, chickens, and people. I closed my eyes. I think he did too!

I recalled this experience, which had prejudiced me forever against horn blowers, as I sat there staring at the sign ahead. Whoever thought up such a bumper sticker anyway? Probably the same person who dreamed up the other one I saw which said, "Warning. This car will be unmanned when the rapture comes." I wondered what kind of witness that could be for such mystified motorists as had not the foggiest as to the meaning of that word so dear to premillennial hearts.

I set my jaw and determined that I was not going to blow my horn. Then I listed my grounds mentally. It was a cheapening of the faith. Anyway, most people love Jesus in one way or another. At present, His is the most admired and popular name in the land. What a racket it would be, then, if all drivers took that bumper sticker seriously. What is more, my little VW Klaxon made a most unenthusiastic squeak. Then, too, what would the lady behind me, who couldn't see the sign ahead, think? She would probably put me down as a son of Jehu.

A made-up mind, however, does not always produce peace of mind. Was the driver ahead concluding from my silence that I was not a Christian? Or, if a Christian, one of those who is afraid to identify himself as one?

What about the Bible? Gabriel has a horn and uses it —or will. The children of Israel blew theirs so mightily that the walls of Jericho collapsed. And didn't the psalmist tell us to make a joyful noise? People in those days sounded off for God with trumpets, lutes, harps, timbrels, and cymbals. Even sackbuts—whatever they were.

It is surprising how many thoughts the human brain can process in just thirty seconds. The sign ahead made me think of some Christians who blow all the time about their love for Jesus. In meetings and in other ways. But nothing more. Quick with tongue, but slow with deed, they make noise for God but little else. Some loud-mouths in the churches have no hands for God, but only fingers wherewith to pinch wallets when Christ's collection plate is passed. Our Master talked to such when He said something like "Why do you blow your horns for me, but do not the things I say?" (Luke 6:46).

55

My thoughts progressed from non-doing blowers to non-blowing doers. I remember the story of The Lady of the Roses. Inactive as a church member, though faithful in attendance, she was one of those silent people who sat afar off from the pulpit. The preacher had her pegged as a mediocre Christian. Confined to her home with a passing illness, the minister made a pastoral call. It was as he had feared. Though friendly, she was not as articulate about her faith as he wished her to be.

Glancing out the window into the backyard, after the manner of one looking for something to say, he discovered her yard ablaze with roses. Commenting on their profusion brought a revelation.

"It is my only talent," said the lady. "I grow them for the Lord. I supply the hospitals with bouquets for patients who otherwise would not receive any. Last week I delivered sixty-six bunches. I guess I overdid and got sick."

The good reverend learned a lesson that day!

The traffic light was about to change. My mood softened toward the bumper sign ahead. After all, it had occasioned a fruitful train of thought. There might even be a sermon idea in it somewhere. As the car in front pulled away, I sounded forth, without conscious decision, two tiny beeps.

The driver waved as he pulled away with the speed of a bigger car.

With my luck, the next light was also red. Again I found myself behind another car and another bumper sticker. This one said, "Summer Stinks. Think Snow." My thoughts, however, were still with the other one. Somewhere between the lights, I had found my text for Sunday's sermon.

Not "Honk if you love Jesus," but similar, though better, words from Christ himself. "If you love me, keep my commandments" (John 14:15).

CABBAGE VERSUS COMPUTER

It was an uneven contest from the beginning—like Jacob wrestling with God. For one thing, my opponent was only twenty-five years old, while I was twice that age. He was baptized ENIAC (Electronic Numerical Integrator and Computer). Born in Philadelphia, Pennsylvania, he weighed thirty tons and was fifteen hundred feet in size. At my birth in Detroit, Michigan, I tipped the scales at less than ten pounds, being only twenty inches long. When we squared off a couple years ago, ENIAC had slimmed down considerably, while I had increased somewhat. Even so, I was by no means his equal.

But if we were a physical mismatch, there was an even greater mental disparity. The simplest of algebraic equations had always baffled me, while my opponent needed only seconds to work problems that would take the brainiest of men lifetimes to solve. What madness, therefore, to challenge him—like David taking on Goliath—especially when the prize for which we were to be locked in combat was a mere two dollars.

It all started when my wife visited a local department store where she purchased a pair of shoes on sale for ten dollars, plus forty cents in tax. Had I known what complications would arise, I would not have admired them as much as I did. For shortly after those shoes walked into my life, ENIAC, who by this time was managing the local department store, plus just about every other business in the country, sent me a bill for twelve dollars and forty cents. This was clearly a two-dollar overcharge. It is true that I had not gone as far in fifty years of life as ENIAC had in twenty-five. He was influential, an international figure of renown, while I was but a lowly, unknown preacher. All the same, I refused to let such comparisons intimidate me. He was wrong and I told him so—by letter.

His reply was as prompt as a right cross responding to a left jab. Out of a long list of alternatives on a form letter, he had marked the one that said, "Check with your local merchant." This proved to be no simple matter. At the general offices, after conferring with several clerks, I was sent to Customer Service, where, after more conferences with more clerks, I was sent to the Shoe Department. There, after a third conference, with still more assorted clerks, I was sent down the street to the local regional office of ENIAC, where, conferring again with many, I was told to mail my ten dollars and forty cents and all would be well. Doing this, ENIAC promptly billed me for the two dollars I had not paid and didn't owe.

Thereupon followed exchanges that shattered my nerves, but not his, for he had none. I told him I owed him nothing. He wrote telling me to check with my local merchant again which, foolishly, I did, going once again through the routine already described, except for the advice which I received at his local regional office, where an attractive clerk spoke soothingly, gave me a glass of water, and told me that though life is tough everywhere, this problem was one I could forget.

The trouble was that ENIAC wouldn't. Dispassionately, coolly, impersonally, he kept sending his statements, adding service charges. I began worrying about my credit rating. I considered sending him the money

I didn't owe in the hope that his ill-gotten gain would prove a curse to him. Instead, I sent him a bill for all the postage my irate letters were costing me, plus damages for wear and tear on my system. I began watching for the mailman so that I could intercept his letters before my wife would see them and become upset. I preached a sermon to my congregation, exhorting them, as good Christians, to let men despitefully use them, feeling hypocritical all the while for not allowing ENIAC to do the same with me. I considered visiting the president of the local department store with the threat that, if he didn't get ENIAC off my back, I would never darken the door of his emporium again. Through it all, ENIAC kept his cool long after I had lost my own. And he just kept sending his diabolical statements, wickedly adding monthly charges.

Then it happened. I was beginning to develop guilt feelings. Though I was clearly in the right, I felt I could no longer look the whole world in the face, unlike the Village Smithy. Particularly when I spied another missive from ENIAC in the mail. I couldn't open it.

But when I finally did, secretly, privately, around midnight, having needed the whole evening to work up the courage, I found inside the envelope a card marked "Final Statement—$00.00." My first impulse was to waken the family with a shout. Instead I settled for a coke.

As I said, it was an uneven contest from the beginning—like Jacob wrestling with God. But Jacob prevailed, and so did I. All the same, I would rather wrestle with his opponent than mine. Jacob received a blessing. I did not. In short, I am glad that God is not a computer (Ps. 103:8-13). Those who say He is are wrong.

CHICKEN LICKEN

Ever since I wrote an article entitled "Bumper Stickers," I have been noticing a proliferation of messages conveyed by the bumpers of America. They are more in number than the signs that scream at motorists from billboards, barns, and fences. Uncounted collisions on the highways have long since demonstrated the uselessness of these chrome protuberances that are supposed to protect our products of Detroit. The modern utilitarian mind has, therefore, put them to work in another way by providing happy motorists with supplementary reading material.

Allow me to digress at this point long enough to say that I am much given to the playing of games when required to do distance driving. Those endless ribbons of cement stretching to infinity, and called expressways, can really dull my mind. In consequence, I often play the alphabet game. One simply looks for an *A* on some sign somewhere, then *B*, and so on to Z. Engaging in this diversionary activity, I find that the letters *J* and *K* are not always readily located. *X*, on the other hand, is an easy letter, what with all the exit signs appearing with monotonous regularity. *Q* is the most difficult of all. One must search diligently, not allowing himself to be diverted from the requirements of good driving, looking for Quality Motel or liquor advertisements to find this rarest letter of them all.

There are other games involving makes of cars, radio programs, counting male versus female drivers, and more in my repertoire. One can play several such games at the same time. But this is not advisable, in view of the fact that one can become so enrapt as to overshoot the mark. A few months ago I became so involved playing three games at once that I traveled a good five miles beyond my point of destination.

My latest invention is to take three bumper sticker signs in a row as I come upon them helter-skelter, stringing them together into some kind of story. Like most of my original ideas, this one, too, doesn't work very well. But the other day it did.

While tooling along the expressway at a modest clip, a lady driver pulled alongside me, and then ahead. She looked prim and proper, and I guessed that if she had any bumper sticker at all, it would probably say "Vote Republican." I went into a slight case of shock and onto the shoulder with two wheels when her bumper became exposed to my vision. She did have a sticker. It said: "If it feels good—do it."

This, I reflected, was a piece of pure hedonism. The good lady was probably driving a vehicle belonging to her errant son. Overcoming a mad desire to ram her backside, thus obliterating a philosophy more befouling to the countryside than her exhaust, I slowed instead for some reflection.

It occurred to me that what I had read represented, in large part, what is wrong with a culture gone crazy. I have never found myself in agreement with those diminishing numbers in this modern world who maintain that if it feels good, it's probably bad. Puritanism has never been my weakness. But I react even more to its opposite. There is a loosening of the moral code. There are countless lives smashed by alcohol and, even more frightening, drugs; many murders are committed because it feels good. Imagine!

But my reverie was interrupted. Another car swept

61

by in pursuit of the proper lady with the improper sign. It, too, had a bumper sticker with a message in announcement form: "The sky is falling."

There came to mind, of course, the good old story of Chicken Licken. I had read it many times to my children when they were small. An acorn fell on Chicken's head and, telling his friends, all went to impart this apocalyptical information to the king.

Strange, I thought. In the past, only preachers spoke of the coming Judgment Day. Today, the scientists and others learned in the ways of nature's resources, ecology and population have assumed the prophet's mantle. At the turn of the century, men believed everything to be getting better—every day, in every way. But today automobiles go scurrying through the countryside scattering the message of Chicken Licken.

And well they might! The sky is indeed falling—and not just because it is heavy with twentieth-century smog. "If it feels good—do it" is an even worse pollutant in the air today, and more dangerous than all the falling acorns in the world put together.

A third car passed me. What message, if any, would it proclaim? Sizing up the driver for a clue left me quite unprepared for what I was about to read. He had a sticker too—not on his bumper, but on his rearview window. It simply said, "Jesus Saves."

I was glad to read it. It gave my thinking a new direction. The Lord saves from the deadly hedonism of the first message I had spied, but also from the dire prophecy of the second.

Lost in reflection, I missed my exit again. Correcting my error at the next exit, I felt it even more important to correct my thoughts. I decided that I had much too quickly interpreted the third sticker in terms of an escape from messages one and two. It is indeed true that Jesus saves from destruction in all its forms. But real evangelical theology asks not only what Jesus saves *from*—but what *for*.

The number of Chicken Lickens is growing. We can join their cackling. We can go and tell the king. We can preach a gospel of escape. A biblical view of the doctrine of election, however, will give us the true perspective. We have been saved; we have been chosen for the Lord's service and healing work, both physical and spiritual, in a world of falling skies.

COMMUNICATION

"The gospel is not communicated because the pulpit does not speak the language of the people." This can't be a very original observation, as I received it from the lips of that eminent churchman, Bishop Robinson. I have heard this line so often that I am in the mood to re-examine this statement which many applaud and accept so readily and uncritically.

I grant that, as preachers, we err when we engage in high-flown phraseology. Some of us would do well to study the *Reader's Digest,* whose secret of circulation must lie, at least partially, in the fact that it presents only such articles as are readily understood by the masses. On the other hand, I believe we insult the intelligence of our listeners when we employ only words of one syllable. The late Gresham Machen balked at dishing out pablum from the pulpit, and he communicated very well. So did Karl Barth, whose sermons were more meat than milk. The fact is that more than any previous generation, this one is highly educated. It is perfectly capable of understanding the deeper aspects of theology, if they are presented with imagination and ability. Perhaps, therefore, some churches which are presently empty would experience an increase in attendance if their pulpits would seek to rise above the levels of Sunday school lessons.

What beats me, however, is the fact that the

preacher is always the whipping boy. He is the one who is everlastingly singled out as the example par excellence of "jargon."

What about the high priests of the Pentagon? Listen to them: "Significant oscillation on indoctrination of non-military personnel using military non-weapons"; "insuperable verification problems on the second strike extenuations"; "deployment subject to redeployment with ceiling intensities."

Or, how about our missionaries into space: "Request go no go instructions on pullout management"; "affirmative acquisition imperative on angulation"; "require communications interface with LMP"; "stomach awareness potential."

Or, once again, how about those bishops of big business: "Upper levels of responsibility in projected actuarial estimates"; "diminishing productions coactive with white paper criteria involvements"; "activities in escalating economic orientations depressing remuneration freezes."

About all I understand in any of this is that somebody feels a bellyache coming on. The doctor's explanation of the symptoms, however, will probably be equally as unintelligible as his prescription will be indecipherable. The truth is that we live in an age of specialization wherein every man views every other man who is not in his own field as a layman. Shall I go on to sound the tongue of the psychiatrist or, that most incomprehensible of all, the language of the teenager? The tower of Babel has never been so high—the anthropologist has his own dictionary, the sociologist another, and so on. What is increasingly needed, it seems, is a linguistic common market.

To the extent that the pulpit engages in this same type of specialeeze, Bishop Robinson is right. But if he means, as I think he does, that the preacher is not communicating when he speaks about justification, forgiveness, sanctification, regeneration, and the like, he is wrong, because these and similar words make up the basic vocabulary of the human heart wherever it is found. When the business executive talks about "actuarial estimates," he is reaching only others in his field, just as the farmer is speaking only to his fellow farmers when he talks about crop rotation. But when a clergyman talks about sin, he reaches even those who deny the word, because all share in the needy condition of the soul. If the church, then, is not communicating in the world today, the solution to the problem must be found along other lines.

The answer, therefore, may well lie in the fact that the church today, in so many places, is not part and parcel of the message it proclaims. The philosopher Nietzche once said, "These Christians must show me they are redeemed before I will believe in their redeemer." Here is a clue to the truth that communication with this age is not, first of all, a matter of language, but life. J. S. Steward points out that when Gibbon attributed the victory of Christianity over the Roman empire to enthusiasm, belief in immortality and miracles, ethics, and organization, he left out the most important thing—the living presence in those who proclaimed the living Christ.

Sometime ago, I attended a service in a foreign land. I couldn't understand a thing. But from the faces of the hearers and the earnestness of the preacher, I got the message loud and clear. So will the world when our lives underwrite our message. We do well to emulate the parson of the town in Chaucer's *Canterbury Tales:*

> But Cristes loore and his apostles twelve
> He taughte, but first he folwed it hymselve.

CRITICISM

I know a preacher who has thin skin. He has thick muscles, ham hands, and a bull neck. He gives the impression of great strength, but it is all negated by thin skin. This is bad because, as any doctor knows, thin skin on the outside leads, eventually, to big ulcers on the inside.

Too bad.

I am thinking, of course, about oversensitivity to criticism. No minister can afford this and live. Instead, he must cultivate a smile on Sunday noons when he knows that here and there some Christian cannibals are having roast preacher for dinner.

Did it ever strike you how conformed we are to the world in this department of life? In pursuance of my task, I am called upon to conduct funerals. Invariably I see a profusion of flowers surrounding caskets. As I appreciate their beauty, I sometimes wonder how many of the floral sprays came too late. Brickbats to the living turn belatedly into bouquets to the dead.

I think of the man who opened a fish market. He had a nice place and it was opening day. Outside he had placed a sign: "Fresh Fish for Sale Here."

He greeted his first customer with a smile. He half anticipated a compliment on his nice place. Instead, the buyer was critical.

"Why does your sign say 'Fresh Fish for Sale *Here?'*

Everybody knows you're not selling them anywhere else." So the owner painted out the word "here."

"Why do you say '*Fresh* Fish for Sale' on your sign?" asked his second customer in a querulous voice. "You wouldn't be selling them if they were not fresh, would you?" So the proprietor altered his sign again, erasing the word "fresh."

"Don't you think it's kind of unnecessary to say 'Fish *for Sale*' on your sign outside?" asked his third customer critically. "Everyone knows a store like yours is for selling." Wearily the man went outside a third time with paint and brush, reducing his sign to just one word—"Fish."

A fourth customer entered. He was as critical as all the others. "Why do you have a sign saying 'Fish'? Everyone knows what you're selling. We can smell them a block away!" By this time, criticism had thoroughly squelched a man who had saved and sacrificed for years to finance this event.

In seminary I heard about the "higher critics." I remember wondering about the necessity of the adjective. So much of what is criticism looks down its nose. This seems especially true in the realm of the church. Of course, there should always be room among us for giving and receiving just criticism. But there is even more room among us for its opposite, which is the compliment.

I am reminded of the housewife who had an unexpected guest. All she had to offer was a piece of pie. It was one of the worst pies she had ever made. To her surprise, the guest not only praised her effort, but did so profusely.

A few weeks later he appeared again, as unexpectedly as before. This time she had one of her best pies in the kitchen—a masterpiece. Yet, though her guest consumed it with relish, he said nothing at all.

"I don't understand," said the hostess. "A few weeks ago I served you a terrible piece of pie and you praised it to the sky. Today I serve you one of the best I ever made and you say nothing at all."

The guest thought for a moment and then said, "Well, you see, that first pie needed praising."

We all need it. We all need compliments and appreciation. We live in an impersonal age which lacks, among other things, the personal touch. Nowadays, we work largely for computers. And computers are cold machines.

When was the last time you gave a pat on the back to your husband or wife, son or daughter, father or mother, pastor, teacher, or friend?

My father was a builder. He was handy with tools. And so, with plenty of tools and wood available, I would sometimes construct boats or birdhouses. But my hands didn't match. I was totally without talent in this regard, whereas my father seemed born with tools in his hands. Nevertheless, I well remember how he would look at my latest monstrosity, full of bent nails, and commend my production.

It made me feel good. I also remember being measured by the kitchen wall and complimented for having grown an inch or two since my last birthday, though I had nothing at all to do with it. That also made me feel warm and secure inside.

It makes me think of our Lord. It is too bad that we so readily see Him as a critical judge rather than as a loving father. We come to Him with our poor bumbling efforts, full of bent nails. Our very best productions must look pathetic in His sight. He would have every reason and every right to be scathing in His criticism.

Instead He says to His children whom He loves, "Well done, thou good and faithful servant."

Imagine! A compliment from God himself!

DELEGATINGMANSHIP

Some years ago Stephen Potter wrote a series of articles, and even books, on such subjects as games-manship, lifemanship, golfmanship, one-upmanship, conversationship, and more. Each of these subjects was projected as a discipline with principles to be mastered and applied. One-upmanship, for example, was de-scribed as that science in which one remained forever ahead of the other fellow—like the proverbial Mr. Jones. The other subjects were similarly presented, in academic fashion, like courses in a college.

It was all, of course, a tongue-in-cheek performance. However, the nomenclature not only stuck, but has today graduated from novelty to idiom. Presently, ref-erences are frequent to brinkmanship, spacemanship, cardmanship, spectatormanship, and more. Recently an article appeared in a newspaper setting forth the fine points of retirementship. It is high time, there-fore, that something be said on another subject not yet delineated—the science of delegatingmanship.

Time was when life was simple. Every man and every family circle was a self-contained unit. Soon enough, however, as Adam's children increased in number, complexities arose. It was found that a man could not do everything. He could not, for example, shear the sheep and at the same time protect the land. It was somewhere at this point that someone—whose name is lost to history—discovered the principle of delegation and thereby conferred a great blessing on us all. God himself had delegated man to "subdue the earth." For man in turn to delegate to fellow-man, in the interests of good order and accomplishment, was merely a refinement of a solid principle. Thus, when the apostles, because of overload, created the office of deacon, shifting certain of their responsibilities into others' hands, the church was able to move forward more efficiently and effectively.

It has remained for the twentieth century, however, to refine a principle into an art. "An executive must know how to delegate authority," it is said. This is true. "In this complicated age no man can hold all the strings." This, too, is true. And so we have come to Organization with a capital "O." And organizational charts, committees, subcommittees, boards, vice-presidents in charge of matters great and small, departments, divisions, echelons, and all manner of wheels and wheels within wheels in the fields of government, business, education, the church, and more. It is all as necessary in today's maze as it is unavoidable. But along with all of this, there has arrived a concomitant: the science of delegatingmanship.

To delegate is to assign a task or duty while retaining the responsibility thereof. As such, it is a legitimate procedure. But delegatingmanship is more. It is of a piece with passing-the-buckmanship. And as such, it has become a state of mind and a way of life—filled with pentagons of secretaries, memos in triplicate, and mountains of tape. Red, that is. All of which has a humorous side. It is a science that has permeated many fields and spheres of human activity, including that of Christian living. It is particularly in the latter area, however, if not in others, that a joke can become a tragedy.

Take Christian education, for example. Parents cannot train the child completely, though before God this is their responsibility. Parents, therefore, seek out other individuals, like-minded and like-committed to the faith of our fathers, and assign to these persons, who are more equipped, the task of teaching the child history, language, arithmetic, and the like. Here is the genesis of the Christian school, and it is based on the sound and solid principle of delegation. In all of this, parents retain the responsibility thrust upon them by their Maker and consciously assumed at the birth of their child.

But see what can happen, and sometimes does. Parents delegate too much. The home abdicates in favor of the school. There is little Christian nurture—if any—in the bosom of the family. It is all left to the Christian teacher (and the preacher). All this is delegatingmanship—a shifting of responsibility. And it is bad.

Or take the missionary program of the church. It grows larger, thankfully. A congregation sends someone to a foreign field to work and witness for the Lord. But in this complex world, the church is not equipped to handle all the details involved in such an undertaking. It has neither the strength nor the talent. And so it delegates. A mission board assumes the details of administration. Well and good.

But again, see what can happen, and sometimes does. The local church falters, till finally it does little more than send a quarterly check to the mission board. Some members of the congregation begin to forget who the missionary is or where he labors. Prayer support, likewise, falls to minimal congregational mission-mindedness, while the one who was sent gradually gravitates more to the board and less to the church. Thus, here again, a virtue has become a vice. The principle of delegation has been abused. There is a word for it: delegatingmanship.

Once more. A minister is called to serve First Church, Midville, U.S.A. He is specifically delegated by ordination and installation to preaching and pastoral activity. However, he soon discovers that more—indeed, much more—is required. Many tasks specifically delegated by God to all Christians are relegated to the clergyman. The Lord says to all his children: "Visit the sick and fatherless." The Lord assigns the task of witnessing to each believer. But all too often these activities, and others, become the exclusive task and sole responsibility of the man in the pulpit. And so here also, as in the other real-life illustrations, too much has been shifted from many to one.

It is good to be alive to the dangers here. Delegatingmanship in the kingdom might yet produce the office of Secretary of Mercy, an administrator in charge of Personal Concern, or a vice-president in charge of Christian Comfort. Farfetched? Perhaps. But in an age of bigness, complexity, impersonalism, professionalism, and specialization, there is increasingly the opportunity to realize the sinful inclination of delegating to others in the kingdom that which God requires of each.

"Letting George do it" manifests such irresponsibility and unconcern as is too much with us, late and soon. But there is something just as bad, or even worse, though on the surface it may seem better, and that is "telling" George to do it when what he is told to do is really something which, before God, should be done by us. This is delegatingmanship. It is on the increase everywhere—even in the church. A delightful art perhaps. Yet deadly for all concerned.

DOWN PEACOCK'S FEATHERS

We had sung a patriotic song and listened to an invocation that was less an offering of petition to God and more an offering of a piece of literature to the audience. We had also polished off a lunch of too many calories and turned our chairs to face the speaker. It was the weekly meeting of a local club, and the guest, whose challenge it was to keep us all awake for the next thirty minutes or so, was being introduced.

I had never heard of him. But apparently I should have, judging from the sheer length of the introduction. All his credentials and accomplishments, however minor, were dragged into the full light of day, volunteered, doubtless, by the speaker himself, who sat basking in their recitation. I couldn't see how he'd ever found time to raise a family. The man was on countless boards and committees. He was active socially and politically on many fronts. In addition, there were his innumerable business involvements, both past and present, and all described for us in minutest detail.

The effect of all of this was both depressing and discouraging to my ego. The more extended the introduction became, the more swollen the speaker appeared, and the more insignificant I felt. Anybody introducing me could do so in less than a minute. In reverie, I began to make up an elongated introduction of myself to an imaginary convocation.

"Ladies and Gentlemen: The speaker I introduce to you today has an impressive academic record. He began his studies at the Berry School in Detroit, Michigan, where he mastered kindergarten under the late Miss McGern, and where he excelled in singing and block building, and where he scored a triumph in the play for the PTA in which, dressed in a policeman's uniform, he blew a whistle. Leaving the Berry School, he went to etcetera, etcetera." By this time, the summation of the credentials of the real speaker before me was finally completed, to which he was responding with a kind of pleased humility. Obviously I was, by this time, in a very critical mood. Fortunately I do have my more charitable days.

But to continue the criticism for a moment, why must prayers be attempted that rival the Gettysburg Address? And why must introductions seek to impress audiences with a speaker's accomplishments exceeding those of the great Saint Paul himself? I recall an occasion when I was to be the speaker. I was introduced as "Doctor" and as a graduate of a certain university of renown. Prefacing my speech with the explanation that I was not a "doctor" and that the closest I had ever come to that certain university of renown was forty miles, I sensed a mood of disappointment in the distinguished audience. In all honesty, however, I must admit that I was disappointed too: that I wished in that magic moment of power that I was a "doctor" indeed; that I had graduated magna cum laude from that university of renown; and that my plain old speech could have been called a lecture. Alas, Absalom was not the only mortal afflicted with the sin of vanity. And Ananias and Sapphira were not the only ones who sought to exaggerate their images.

Speaking of images, I learned years ago from an older and more experienced minister how to inflate my own if I so desired. He considered his name, which was John Smith, to be an intolerable handicap to him in his climb in the ecclesiastical world. Fortunately he had, if not a glamorous, then, certainly, an uncommon middle name. Accordingly, the bulletin board outside his church, as well the bulletins inside, announced him as the Reverend J. McDermit Smyth. In his opinion, I would go much farther and be more impressive, he said, if capitalizing on my middle name, I would advertise myself as the Reverend J. Dirk Eppinga. I must say that since learning of this shortcut to prestige, I have noticed, from various bulletin boards across the country, that my friend was not the only one to ride this ruse.

But lest anyone thinks that only preachers are liable to such temptations, let me say that I once knew a guy named "Pete" who became "Pierre" upon graduating from barber's college. I also know another fellow whose walk would take on a little swagger each time he went to the local lodge where he wore a ceremonial apron, a silly hat, and where he was known as "the grand superior potentate," or something. The long and the short of it is that we all preen our feathers and, like Paul before he knew better, catalogue our distinctions for all to hear (Phil. 3:5, 6). It started with Lucifer, I suppose, who, through pride, wanted to be more than he was, thereby falling to considerably less than what he could have been.

All of which brings us to a lesson found in "The Misery of Man" in the Anglican Book of Homilies. ". . . wherefore, good people, let us beware of such hypocrisy, vain glory, and justifying of ourselves. Let us look upon our feet: and then down peacock's feathers, down proud heart, down vile clay, frail and brittle vessels."

DO YOURSELF A FAVOR

A good letter can make your day. This week the mailman delivered a dandy. It was from a young lady who is presently involved in summer mission work. She is enthusiastic about what she is doing.

"Funny," she writes, "when I was in catechism class I couldn't wait for the season to end. But now that I am teaching a group of children myself, I enjoy both preparing and presenting each Bible lesson. I'm probably getting more out of it than the kids."

Her candor brings a universal experience into focus. The Dead Sea is dead because it keeps what it gets. The Sea of Galilee, on the other hand, is a living body because, as has been pointed out in countless homilies, it allows the waters it receives to pass through. I'm sure Jesus said it best when He pointed out that though it is a blessing to receive, it is a greater blessing to give.

I remember those piano lessons of years ago. My father had decreed that I should master that instrument. Accordingly, I was practicing my scales long before my legs could reach the pedals.

What a shame that my otherwise clear sky had to have this dark cloud in it. Practicing half an hour each afternoon was, in the parlance of today, a real drag. There was no way to speed the minutes, each one of which lasted an hour. Moving the clock ahead didn't work at all, though I tried occasionally. The discovery

77

Of Cabbages and Kings

of this unworthy ruse resulted unfailingly in doing extra time on the bench.

My teacher, Miss Czarnet, always seemed to show up just when it was my turn at the plate in the alley where we played ball. It was torture to drop the bat, the passion of my life, and come into the house, where I had to sit on that bench so close to a member of the opposite sex who smelled of perfume. The fact that she always munched on candy bars while I struggled with the lesson didn't help much easier.

It wasn't that I was completely devoid of talent. There were times when she pasted a gold star in the book as a reward for work well done. There was even a sense of accomplishment in being a part of the annual Sunday school program, pounding out "O Little Town of Bethlehem," with variations, including the feat of crossing my hands and playing the melody in the lower register. Yet even this was not sufficient reward for offsetting the taunts of some friends who insisted that piano playing was for girls.

If I dwell on all of this, it is only to underline a contrast with what follows. Still practicing, but now in high school, it occurred to me that I might well turn my past agonies into some material profit by becoming a teacher of piano. There seemed incidental justice, too, in inflicting on others that which I had been made to bear.

Sharing my plan, but not my motivations, with my father brought a positive response. Liking my spirit of enterprise, he fashioned a "shingle," which he promptly nailed to the front of the house. Soon I had ten pupils, which, at fifty cents a head a week, brought some nifty pocket money in what was now "the depression."

Then a strange thing happened. Gradually, I fell in love. With the piano! The more I taught others, the more interested I became myself. The more I insisted that they practice, the more I practiced myself. Music became my life. I branched out into the violin and the

78

trumpet. I discovered the Detroit Symphony Orchestra. I vowed I would become a musician.

The fact that I eventually became a preacher instead is no evidence of a subsequent disaffection. No Paderewski, I still love the piano and spend time with it.

My experience with the eighty-eight ivories is the same as that of the young lady of the letter with the Sixty-six Books. Passing along what she has received is making it all new and alive. Those who listen to sermons on Sundays and then go out to "witness" know what I mean.

"This church has a money box at the door, son. Whatever the people put in is for the preacher." The visiting clergyman was pointing it out to his small boy, who was accompanying his father on a preaching assignment. The minister put in a dime, explaining that afterward he would get it back, together with whatever else the people might contribute.

Afterward, when the box was emptied, only the dime fell out. Whereupon the youngster made an observation containing more truth than he knew.

"Well, dad," he said, "I guess you get out of it what you put into it." Only receiving in the pew is not yet "putting in." So the next time somebody asks you to teach a Sunday school class, or whatever, do yourself a favor.

EMERGENCY!

I have much admiration for the little Dutch boy, of legendary fame, who put his finger in the hole in the dike. He had presence of mind. It is a quality I lack. Under similar circumstances, I would have gone scurrying for a bucket or something. My intentions would be commendable, but they would be exceeded by my stupidity. The truth is that I am not your man in an emergency. It's not that I freeze in the face of impending calamity. On the contrary, I fly into action. But I always do the wrong thing.

There was that day we had a fire in the kitchen. My father and I were home alone. He was cooking our evening meal, and I was helping. Some grease spilled. A fire began. There was a lot of smoke. The curtains were in flames.

I was almost glad it had happened, having just read an article on how to avoid the dangers of smoke inhalation. Rushing to the bathroom, soaking a towel and covering my nose with it, I returned to the kitchen, assuming a prone position on the floor. There, so the book said, the smoke would be less dense. It was the thing to do. Meanwhile, my father was rushing about, being careful not to step on me, in his frantic but successful efforts in single-handedly smothering the flames.

In my adult years, sadly, I have not improved. There was that time our dog had a seizure. My children rushed to her side. I helped too, or thought I did, by dashing into the living room to shut off the radio. Or there was that other time when someone was going to faint. My reflexes were instant. Sprinting for the kitchen, I came back with a pan.

How do you administer mouth-to-mouth resuscitation? Being that same person who in earlier years tried to inform himself on the proper deportment in the presence of a fire, I have read articles on how to rescue the perishing in rivers and lakes and have even attended rescue demonstrations. Yet if questioned at this moment, I would fail this part of the lifesaver's examination.

Each time I was about to become a father, I was careful to consider the possibility of not making it to the hospital. Accordingly, each time the blessed event was approaching, I hauled a book out of the library, propping *How to Deliver a Baby* up on the shelf next to *Berkhof's Dogmatics.* Assiduously I studied both the intricacies of midwifery and Reformed doctrine. I could call on some knowledge of the one in the pulpit. I am sure that in a car, my mind would have drawn a complete blank on the other.

It all adds up to a standing in awe of doctors and nurses who meet emergencies every day and measure up to them. I also think of a gallant and courageous little lady who is a missionary in Barillas, Guatemala, and who functions amazingly as the town doctor with no training. Just a *Home Medical Guide.*

Policemen and firemen, too, have my utter respect. I pray for them and I thank God for them. I remember a wild night in a police cruiser. Officer Pierce, awarded a Congressional Medal of Honor in the war, was equal to every emergency. He broke into a gambling house at 5 A.M. in search of a thief who had just robbed the corner store. From the outside, the house appeared dark and even uninhabited. Before entering, he said he would be going directly upstairs in search of the culprit. He said I should remain downstairs and pretend to be a plainclothesman until more help arrived. To my amazement, there was a room filled with unsavory characters. I promptly announced to them, in stentorian tones, that, in my opinion, it was about to snow.

The next day the *Press* announced on page one that a local clergyman had assisted in an arrest—which merely proves you can't believe everything you read in the newspapers.

Speaking of the fourth estate, I read a news item a long time ago about a mother who, without help, lifted a piano that had tipped over, imprisoning the arm of her child. More recently, I read of another young lady, barely one hundred and twenty pounds, pushing a car right side up. It had overturned at a curve in the road with its occupants inside and unable to escape. These instances, I am told, prove what people can do in dire circumstances.

People—yes. But don't place any bets on me. Bets are wrong. And, on me, foolish.

However, it is a mystery how so many who cope with smaller emergencies engage in so many wrong and ineffectual efforts with respect to The Great Emergency. I am thinking of the national and international straits we are in, the sickness afflicting our society in particular and all of mankind in general. All sorts of cultural, political, and economic salves are being applied. In frenetic haste, many run from pan to bucket. Others are passing out wet towels in a world of flame. The activism is commendable. Yet so much that is being done is about as effectual as turning a radio dial for a dog in a fit.

I am sorry that I strike out so often in so many emergencies.

In facing The Great Emergency, however, I am convinced that I am doing the right thing.
I am preaching the Gospel.
What are you doing?

EMPATHY

The other day a man told me that I couldn't possibly understand what it is like to be a salesman, as he is, in the competitive world of business that is his. He went on to refer to all my colleagues who, he said, "just don't understand." He made it rather obvious that he was down on clergymen. My first reaction was an impulse to inform him that I wasn't born yesterday, that I knew a thing or two myself, and that I had more acquaintance with more aspects of life than he seemed willing to admit. But I thought better of it. So instead of challenging his statement, I allowed it to stand. I did this because basically, all recrimination aside, the man was absolutely right. I do not understand what it is like to be a salesman in the competitive world of business that is his.

On the other hand, he has no idea what it is like to be a preacher. Had I told him that, I too would have been absolutely right. By all of which we are reminded of an important fact of existence. Contrary to John Donne's poem, there is a sense in which every man is, indeed, an island, difficult to reach, and impossible fully to explore. We hear a lot about empathy today —the imaginative projection of one's own consciousness into another's being. This, however, is a difficult thing to do. In the complete sense it is, in fact, impossible. Cabbages do not know what it is to be kings

(2 Kings 6:30), and vice versa. Yet the more we try to empathize, the more we understand each other and the less we are ready to condemn. "Don't judge another man until you have walked in his shoes for thirty days" is a proverb as wise as it is ignored.

Those who wish to take this saying seriously, in their effort to make the world a better place, might well think about Walter Mitty, George Plimpton, and John Howard Griffin—in that order. Walter Mitty had imagination. While running errands for his wife in henpecked fashion, he fancied himself, with crystal clarity, as all sorts of people: a commander of a navy hydroplane in trouble; a famous surgeon operating on a millionaire who was afflicted with obtreosis of the ductal tract; a fearless British pilot with a Webley-Vickers automatic strapped on; a prisoner facing the firing squad, standing proud and undefeated, shoulders back, heels together, smoking a cigarette, and refusing a blindfold. Exposing Mitty's heroic secret existence, the author, James Thurber, drew a slice of life.

George Plimpton, however, had more than just imagination. Instead of merely fancying himself a member of a symphony orchestra or a baseball or football team, he actually undertook all of these roles personally. He practiced the triangle as if his life depended on it, so that he might "ping" just right and at the proper second for a demanding Leonard Bernstein. He exercised his arm so that he could throw in a game for the New York Yankees. And in his book *Paper Lion*, he revealed something of the rigors of the football world as, with nerve mingled with curiosity, he landed on a Detroit roster as a rookie quarterback.

But the late John Howard Griffin went even further. Mitty and Plimpton played roles, one in fancy and one in fact, that were attractive to them. Griffin, however, darkened his skin, crossed the color line, and lived as a Negro, looking for food and rest and feeling the

85

weight of hopelessness that rests so heavily on the shoulders of Afro-Americans. In *Black Like Me,* he reported his troubling story, burning it deeply into the consciousness of us all.

Perhaps these three examples, when put together, can show us the way to greater empathy. With the imagination of a Mitty, the application of a Plimpton, and the dedication of a Griffin, I might more deeply come to appreciate what life is like for my salesman acquaintance and, thus, more fully understand the man himself. "In a fractured humanity," said a wise old sage, "what is needed is for every man to try to get into the skin of another." Or, as a psychiatrist pointed out recently, role-switching, as practiced sometimes in group therapy, increases understanding of the other fellow's problems.

In the ultimate sense, of course, there is only One who could and who did take our skin upon himself. Not just a God of sympathy, He went way beyond empathy, becoming "like unto us." In His spirit we ought, at least, to try projecting ourselves into other's shoes. Perhaps we shall not only gain understanding, but by doing so, win others to the faith.

FIDO

The cheetah, the polar bear, the wolf, and some other species of animals are nearing extinction. I hope their population decline can be reversed. Meanwhile, I am thankful that my favorite animal, the dog, is in no such peril.

As a boy, it used to bother me that I could find no favorable references to dogs in the Bible. I was sure that when Adam named all the animals, he must have noticed that there was as great a difference between the canine and all other creatures as between the canine and himself. It helped a little when it was pointed out to me that the biblical references were mostly to scavengers who, to this day, roam the East, singly and in packs. Accordingly, the citizens of Constantinople, for example, hold the world of dogdom in low esteem. Relations between our countries were not helped when, as happened years ago, an American first-grade primer fell into the hands of a Pasha. On the first page there appeared a picture of a dog, and under it an inscription: *This is my dog. His name is Turk.*

Amid the forty or so uncomplimentary biblical references to man's best animal friend, there was at least one, however, that warmed my boyish heart. What made it even better was that it came from the lips of Jesus. In telling the story of the rich man and Lazarus, he said that the dogs came and licked Lazarus' sores.

What a miserable rich man that was to let a poor fellow in such condition sit out on the sidewalk! But how nice that he had the companionship of such animals as the rich man could never match in compassion! Whenever father read that story at the table, I always sneaked an extra leftover under it for the mutt we owned and loved.

But if it disturbed me to discover a paucity of good dogs in the Good Book, it upset me even more to learn that they had no souls. I remember the day when the matter was thoroughly aired in catechism class. I'm afraid I must admit that, at the time, my interest on this question surpassed the attention I gave to higher doctrines. If a covenant God loved believers and their children, wouldn't He love their children's pets as well? Couldn't they have some kind of heaven too? I was grateful to my teacher, who had the sensitivity to avoid both heresy in himself and a negative reaction in me. True, he didn't quite meet the issue head-on. But he did speak of a world in which Christ made all things new and of a day when the lion and the lamb would lie down together. It was enough to satisfy me for the moment.

But if dogs do not have souls, they do, indeed, have gods. I remember a collie to whom I was the deity incarnate. He had no will of his own—only mine. More faithful than my shadow, he was with me in the dark as well as day. He sensed my moods more expertly than the most perceptive child psychologist. He was more eloquent with his tail than the preacher on Sundays with his mouth. He was ready for play when I was ready and willing to wait when I was sick. He was a worthy forerunner of my present slave and servant, Pal, who is always at the door to welcome me returning from a lengthy consistory meeting, long after the rest of the family has retired.

Surely a Christian world and life view must include a kindly pat on the heads of the Fidos of the world, so many of whom have rescued children from drowning, mountaineers from danger, dragged men's burdens, and man himself in the polar and other regions of the earth. Children often sense the worth of this creature of God more readily than their parents.

I remember a day in the country with some cousins years ago. We came upon a mangy hound too sick to move his tail, let alone his feet. As we carried him home to deposit him in the living room of my super housekeeper aunt, one of my cousins ventured the opinion that God would surely like us a little more for our deed-in-process. The thought made us feel that we were real Christians in action as well as by belief.

When Auntie saw the occupant of her embroidered chair, she yelped in pain and told us to get that fleabag out of there. At that moment my estimation of her plummeted like the stock market of 1929. But it went right up again when, moments later, she appeared solicitously on the back porch with a bowl of milk for the object of our Christian act. The memory of this incident has always reminded me that an effective witness to the little ones involves a love for whatever pets they have. Often children judge their superiors by their attitude to the children's inferiors.

But why am I writing all this? Dogs are neither cabbages nor kings, though they serve both well. By this time, some reader may be thinking that this book is going to the dogs. Worse things could happen.

I am writing this because the other day I saw that old victrola ad of years ago: a dog seated before an old-style speaker with these words underneath: *His Master's Voice.* Would that we listened to our Master's voice as much.

And I am writing this because of a book of animal prayers I had in hand some time ago. It included the prayer of the dog: "Dear Lord, only You and I know what faithfulness is."

F.O.B. DETROIT

It was the last straw. I went right out to the garage and gave my left rear tire a kick. I had been watching a television show, during which the commercial plugged the virtues of a certain automobile. The last straw was when the announcer said that this particular car had sex appeal. Sex appeal!?

Henry Ford influenced my life even before I was born. Had the motor city not been booming by way of his production lines, my parents might have lived elsewhere. As it was, I first saw the light of day smogged by smokestacks giving birth to Hupmobiles.

I was five years old when my father came home with our first car. That put me one up on my friend Stanley White, whose father couldn't afford one. Shortly thereafter, his dad got one too and had a flat tire on the first day. That put Stanley one up on me. But not for long, because soon after, my father had an accident with ours. This was the ultimate distinction. Stanley deprecated this. He said it wasn't a real accident because it had been caused by a black cat crossing my father's path and, therefore, didn't count.

When I was a little older, I became an expert on cars, along with the averages of baseball players. I could identify Marmons, Reos, LaSalles, and all the others at great distances. The Marmon was the first to come out with a rear view mirror—nice, but totally unnecessary.

Occasionally we took trips of great distances to Kalamazoo or Grand Rapids. This necessitated early retirement the night before so that we could be off at the break of day. These interminable journeys were frequently punctuated by my questions of, "Are we almost there?" and stops at those four-by-four comfort stations that stood nakedly against countryside backdrops behind schoolhouses.

I witnessed the first sit-down strike in history. It happened at Chrysler, a mile or so from where we lived. People stood on Jefferson Avenue watching the workers waving from the windows. I gave one a candy bar and felt guilty afterward for having supported such lawlessness with my gift.

When I entered junior high, my father said I should enroll in the practical arts course because "every boy must learn a trade." This put me in something called "auto shop," which I hated and failed. Then, as now, I could do nothing more than stare at motors uncomprehendingly.

I bought my first car in partnership with a high school chum. It was an old clunker for which we each paid $2.50. It didn't work. My pastor came over in old clothes, crawled underneath, and fixed it. It was amazing what this did for my view of ministers. Thereafter I listened to him on Sundays with new respect.

When I went to college I bought an old Overland for $40. It gave ten miles for every quart of oil. Along with fouling the air, it was beginning to dawn on me that my original $2.50 investment in the motor millennium was adding up. Even so, I had no notion as to the financial drains ahead. My first real car was a Studebaker. I named it Rachel because it took me (Jacob) fourteen years of work to pay for it, which is only a slight exaggeration.

F.O.B. stands for free-on-board. This is a misnomer.

There is nothing free about our modern means of transportation. But, then, there was nothing free about the old means either. I found an ancient church budget the other day. It contained an item of $80—feed for the minister's horse.

He polluted the countryside too. The horse, I mean.

When I try to assess the influence of the automobile, I falter. It is simply immeasurable. I can only touch a piece of this subject by suggesting three areas out of many: sermons, myself, and others.

Take sermons, for example. When I was a boy, the automobile made its presence felt in our pulpit. The minister spoke often of the evils of Sunday joy-riding. Today, if the automobile is mentioned at all in the pulpit, it is to deplore the carnage on the highways and the pollution of the air. The old phrase, "Sunday joy-riding," falls unrecognized on the ears of the young. Chalk up a point for the car over the Sabbath.

As for the motor industry in its influence on me, it was there before I was born. Has Christ influenced my life as much?

As for others, I trust that not too many will fall for that television ad about sex appeal. Those who do should remember the old adage that "Things are to use; people are to love." There are those who get this confused. The more's the pity. For loving things leads to using people. It is a characteristic of a materialistic age.

GOD'S JEWELRY

I have read the Bible from cover to cover many times. Even so, I am always making new discoveries in it—reading things I never noticed before.

It happened again the other day. I saw Titus 2:10 as if for the very first time. It is a verse which talks about the fact that we should adorn the doctrine of God our Savior. It made me think of some who wish to do away with doctrine. I also considered others who, at the opposite extreme, seem to find the essence of Christianity in mere subscription to doctrine. Persuing my private devotions, I had another idea. How wonderful, I thought, that our Lord should even believe it possible that sinful people can be ornaments of truth!

Can clay adorn the ruby? Can a broken vessel embellish the diamond?

*   *   *

I should have made the call a week ago. It was a poor excuse to say that I had been too busy with church committee meetings, sermons, and counseling. This was true enough, as well as the fact that there are only so many hours in a day. However, I could not escape the feeling that I had been remiss.

The doorbell was out of order. So were some other things ever since her husband had been institutionalized. With limited means and bent with arthritis, she found it difficult to tend to things. But she wanted no help. She always said that there were others who were in far greater need. Responding to my knock, she ushered me into her living room, spare yet neat.

I received the usual reception—like I was royalty. I shouldn't have bothered to come. I had more important things to do. I should have some tea and a biscuit. And when on earth was I ever going to take a much-needed vacation? She prescribed Florida, a place she had never seen.

They were providing wonderful care for her husband. Those nurses were just about the dearest things in all the world. No, she didn't need a thing. God was providing, and her cup was running over, she said, as she filled mine with more tea. And how was my wonderful family?

After prayer, I left, feeling that I had received far more than I had brought.

I wasn't thinking of the beverage and the biscuit.

* * *

They were a young couple, much in love and on vacation. It was Sunday and they were on their way to church. But the church was far away, and the traffic was as heavy as the weather was hot.

They knew it was risky to pick up a stranger. But the middle-aged man extending his thumb seemed to be melting in the sun. They hesitated, then stopped.

For the next several miles they conversed with him across the great cultural and social distances that separated them. They also witnessed to the love of God.

Their passenger, whose language was rough without being coarse, spoke of his broken home. He grew wistful as he saw how beautiful, by contrast, the relationship of his young hosts appeared. It also seemed unusual to him that his benefactors were rushing so—to get to church, of all things! And places!

"Say a prayer for me when you get there," he said as he stepped out, adding, "I can sure use one."

"We think the Lord would want us to give this to you," said the driver. "Here. We were going to put it in the collection plate."

The man watched them as they sped off, holding God's offering in his hand.

A five-dollar bill.

❋   ❋   ❋

He was always in church. Twice each Lord's Day.

"A man has to fill his place in this world," he said. "And this is my place each Sunday," he added, gesturing towards the sanctuary from which he had just emerged.

There were those who were critical of him. For one thing, he never sang the hymns.

"I can't sing," he said simply. "It would bother others. So, I sing inside of me."

There were those who thought that he should take part in the activities of the church. They had little understanding of the fact that his shyness was so painful to him that he considered it his cross. Indeed, so far as he could see, there was only one thing he could do for his Lord, and that he did. That's why I saw him every Lord's Day—twice.

There came a Sunday afternoon when the air was heavy with evil portent. It was a tornado watch. The evening service was automatically canceled.

I went to church anyway. There could be some who had missed the announcement, even though it was being repeated on the radio with great frequency.

One came. The silent one. Yes, he had heard about the tornado watch. But he had forgotten about our policy of automatic cancellation of services under such conditions.

"But didn't you think of your safety?" I asked.

"A man has to fill his place," he said. "And this is

my place each Sunday," he added, gesturing towards the empty sanctuary.

We had a visit and a prayer.

In the basement.

✿   ✿   ✿

She was new in the neighborhood, coming to church regularly even though she spoke and understood English poorly. She also manifested a reverence for me and the church, so characteristic of some who come from eastern Europe.

She came on Thursday morning to give me fifty cents.

"Please, Reverend sir, every third Sunday I work in the hospital. Next Sunday is third Sunday. I bring offering now."

For a long time thereafter she came every Thursday morning before the third Sunday.

To bring her offering.

✿   ✿   ✿

Can clay adorn the ruby? Can a broken vessel embellish the diamond? As I think of how an arthritic, a young couple, a man who fills his place, and a cleaning lady adorn the doctrine of God our Savior, I make Gypsy Smith's song my prayer.

For this is the way to Titus 2:10: "Lord, let the beauty of Jesus be seen in me."

HOUSE OF EARTH

I remember one of the cheapest and best vacations I ever had. My friend and I pooled our resources and purchased an entire automobile, all for the grand sum of five whole dollars. In an alley somewhere we found a discarded storefront awning out of which we fashioned what we called (and what everyone else did not recognize) a tent. An uncle of my friend, who owned a grocery store, donated a small case of canned pork and beans. Packing these, along with some sugar and Kool-Aid, we set out on a camping trip. Fifty miles, twelve hours, and ten flat tires later found us beside a wonderful lake, where, pitching our sorry shelter, we felt like kings. Cold pork and beans for breakfast, washed down with Kool-Aid, subtracted absolutely nothing from the grand experience. Anyway, this fare was soon supplemented by the fat, fresh, and sassy bluegills we pulled out of a liquid world, so pure it seemed untouched by sin.

All this was only yesterday. Today, I had the opportunity to visit again this site upon which we once erected a leaky canvas. I wish I hadn't. The lake is more sewer than lake. Urban sprawl has cursed the land. There's all the difference there between today and yesterday as exists between Genesis one and three. The "No Fishing" notice seems superfluous as, I am sure, the progeny of the fish we caught have long since been squeezed into oblivion by their own increasingly uninhabitable environment.

What has happened to them seems to be happening to us. For the lake revisited is only a picture of our plight in microcosm. With an oil slick here and a junk pile there; here some smoke, there some pollution; everywhere smog and filth—Old MacDonald's earth isn't what it used to be.

I find myself looking at Romans 8:22 with a deeper insight gained from the perspective of today's earth, soiled and tired. Without staking my name as an exegete on this point, I do think that because of our indifference to our dwelling place, "the whole creation groaneth and travaileth in pain" a little more. God's cursing of the ground (Gen. 3:17) seems small indeed compared with man's. The latter, by avarice and greed and all his other sins, has fouled his nest to an alarming extent.

Is there a sin against creation? The first commandment that we love God would seem to imply caring for that which He has made. My bookcase gets all the more loving attention simply because my father built it once upon a time. In the same way, it seems to me that Christians would wish to treat what their heavenly Father has made with extra affection. Yet it is our Christian (Western) culture that has scuffed up the furniture of our earthly house so badly, and this in spite of the fact that God told us to take good care of His handiwork. At least this is what I think He was saying when in Leviticus 25, as well as other places, He told us to avoid tiring the earth.

Is there a theology of environment? The second great commandment would seem to indicate as much. It is impossible to love one's neighbor and choke him to death at the same time by poisoning the wind. The Lord "renewest the face of the earth" (Ps. 104:30) for the benefit of all. Whatever we do in an opposite direction is to the detriment of all and evidence of the absence of the concern we owe each other.

Our House of Earth needs cleaning and repair. There is dirt on the carpet and dust in the air. The overflowing contents of the garbage can are threatening to engulf the yard. The pipes are rusty and polluted, and the plumbing needs an overhaul. The debris brooding upon the face of the waters in the garden is surely not the Spirit of God, nor is that black pillar of cloud rising from the chimney. Maybe cleanliness is not next to godliness. But in the list of priorities for the well-being of our House of Earth, it seems exactly that.

HYPERBOLE

"The sermon was so long my ten-year-old was an inch taller by the time we sang the doxology."

"The minister was so thin he was invisible when you looked at him sideways."

Who says I never learned anything in high school! For one thing, I became knowledgeable in figures of speech. I could identify the above sentences as hyperbole. I learned about similes and metaphors. Onomatopoeia is a literary device which adapts the sound to the sense. Hyperbole is exaggeration for effect. I got "A" in all this stuff.

Some people are much given to hyperbole, though they may never have heard of the word. Years ago I had a friend who went to visit New York City. He came back and told me that the Empire State building was a million miles tall. When we came home from the circus one day, he told my parents that we had seen the fat lady. He informed my father that she weighed a hundred thousand tons—not one ounce less. I learned from my association with him that there are people in this world whose words must be cut in half. I was fully persuaded that the fat lady weighed only fifty thousand tons.

I find quite a bit of hyperbole in the Bible. There were those spies in the Old Testament who went out to appraise the Promised Land. When they returned, they told the Israelites that the cities they had seen were walled to heaven and the inhabitants so tall that they were as grasshoppers in their sight. And I recall David's lament over Saul and Jonathan. He said that they had been "swifter than eagles and stronger than lions." I'm sure he didn't mean that literally. He was just trying to get a point across. So he exaggerated—for effect.

In my view, God himself used hyperbole. He told Abraham that He would make His seed like the dust of the earth and like the stars of the heavens. But, then, maybe somebody would give me an argument on this one.

I find exaggeration used as a figure of speech in the New Testament as well. When Jesus talked about stones crying out in the wilderness, and when He said something about a camel and a needle, He was using extreme language in order to make His point. And how about John, the disciple, when he said that if everything Jesus said and did in His earthly ministry were written down, even the world itself would not be able to contain the books that would be published?

Because I find hyperbole used as a figure of speech in the Bible, I dare to use it myself. If you ask me about my trip to Europe some years ago, I will tell you that the Rhineland is paradise, and that Cambridge, England, is the greatest town in all the world, and that any Frisian farmhouse exceeds the Taj Mahal in beauty. It is wrong to say the fish I caught measured twenty inches when, in fact, it was undersize. That is lying. But hyperbole bears no false witness. Instead it registers truth, for it is indeed a fact that the Rhineland is a garden, and that Cambridge is exceeding fair, and that a Dutch farmhouse is a thing of quiet dignity.

"So what else is new?" you ask. Well, you see, I am trying to get at St. Paul. A few years ago I wrote a little book about him. In preparation for that effort,

101

I sat down and read all that he had written in the New Testament, from Romans to Philemon, in one sitting. A few evenings later I did this again. Altogether, I read Paul from start to finish twenty times. Doing this, I gathered such impressions and feelings as are almost impossible to gain by way of reading Scripture in my usual little bits and pieces. For one thing, there came through to me the fact that Paul sounded more hyperbolical than anybody I had ever read. I was struck with the ever-recurring extremity of his language.

"I am persuaded that neither death nor life . . . Christ, the dynamite of God . . . if Christ is not risen, we are of all men most miserable . . . crucified with Christ . . . a new creature . . . there is therefore now no condemnation . . . I count everything but dung" . . . etc., etc.

Paul never wrote calmly. He taxed the dictionary to the limit. Reading him all the way through again and again, I felt like telling him to calm down. I felt like reminding him that he was over fifty. I felt like warning him that he might have a heart attack writing the way he wrote. "Eye hath not seen, nor ear heard. . . ." Paul sounded like a Hollywood agent who describes every pictures as superterrific and the film of the century.

All of which brings me back to my friend of former years. He spoke so consistently in hyperbole that I had to cut everything he said in half, and then some. Must I do the same with Paul? Does he consistently exaggerate for effect, or is everything he says stone cold sober truth?

In short, is the gospel hyperbole? The fact is that it is not. John 3:16 stretches absolutely nothing.

But if it doesn't—

How is it that you are so calm about it all!?

NOTICE! COMMITTEE MEETING AT EIGHT!

I remember my first committee meeting. Since then I have gone to a million. Our fathers were always off and running to these affairs when we were boys. What they did, once there, was a considerable mystery to us. We could tell from their faces, though, that these were important things. My father was a member of the Building Committee of the Consistory. Don's dad was chairman of the Parks Committee for the city, while Mr. Schoenborn, Clarence's progenitor and an enthusiastic lodge member, went to a committee meeting practically every night. We argued some as to which of our fathers belonged to the most important, though we were sure they all were that, since these committees occupied so much of our fathers' energies. And so it was inevitable, I suppose, all of us being father-admirers, that one of us, I forget which, came up with the utterly stupendous idea that we should have a committee too.

First of all we needed a place. Private. Away from inquisitive mothers. So we scoured alleys for materials out of which to construct a place of meeting on a vacant lot. We enlisted the help of friends. For a reward, we promised that they, too, could be members of the committee. When our structure was completed, we all crawled on our bellies through the inadequate entrance, taking care not to bump the low and precarious ceiling with our heads. Inside we lay in a circle, solemnly facing one another in dim light and in the closest of quarters. The Committee!

The first thing we did was select a chairman. This was accomplished with no difficulty and absolutely no objections. The biggest was the chairman. The selection of the assistant chairman was no problem either. The best friend of the biggest was the assistant chairman. Nobody wanted to be secretary. Secretaries were girls. We didn't know if we needed a treasurer, like in a club, but if we did, the chairman who was the biggest would be the treasurer too.

What followed hereupon I have always remembered. Having taken care of the organizational aspect of our committee, no one knew what came next. We had no agenda—a situation I have since endured more than once. Children, however, are more direct than adults. The latter are really much better at playing games and pretending. Sometimes we grown-ups conduct business when there is really no business to conduct. A dozen small boys leaning on their elbows! One long pause, and then the chairman spoke. "Committees," he said, "stink." Whereupon the first one I was ever on dissolved.

Actually, however, they don't. It is true that the jokes we make about them are often deserved. A camel is a horse put together by a committee. Committees are more repetitious than the spelling of the word. A committee keeps minutes and wastes hours. The most effective committee is made up of three people, one of whom is sick, and the other out of town. A committee is a way of postponing a decision. A committee is a group of people who individually can do nothing and who collectively decide nothing can be done. Fred Allen often cut Congressional committees down to size with similar jibes, while Robert Benchley with his "The Treasurer's Report" and other pieces could hold committees up to good-natured ridicule. Yet, when all is said and done, what would we do without them?

While eating in a restaurant a few weeks ago, I could not help overhearing four men in an adjoining booth discussing the finances of their church. It soon became apparent that they were a committee and were sharing their lunch hour discussing the King's business. "How fine," I thought. For breakfast, lunch, dinner, during evenings, and sometimes far into the night, and all over the land, the committees labor on to keep the wheels of the church in motion. Many things die in committee. Yet much emerges, too, thanks to those uncounted and unsung committee members who are so willing to give their time and do their best.

It is well, upon occasion, to peruse the backs of church bulletins, to see the committees listed there, and to breathe a twofold word of thanks: first of all, gratitude for their existence; and second, thanksgiving for the fact that John 3:16 reads the way it does. For God so loved the world that He didn't send a committee.

OSCAR

It never happened, of course. And yet it sort of
happens, here and there, quite frequently. The Academy of Ecclesiastical Awards was holding its annual
bash. All the nominees were present in their clerical
attire, accompanied by wives wearing anxious smiles.
Throughout the year competition had been keen for
the gold-plated oscars made of zinc. Former recipients
had discovered that these were, indeed, worth their
weight in true gold in terms of calls, promotions, and
the like. A few had even had their trophies perma-
nently and conspicuously positioned in their pulpits.
Saturday church ads were useful, too, in identifying
various members of the cloth as "nominated for five
academy awards," "winner of two academy awards,"
et cetera.

Proceedings commenced sharply at 10 p.m., as previously arranged with the television network, which
had promised that everyone would get in the picture.
The orchestra opened with a mishmash of traditional
and contemporary hymns, the melodies being played
alternately by organ and guitar. It was deemed a nice
touch, designed to satisfy all tastes.

The podium, naturally, had the contours of a pulpit.
The carvings on three sides were magnificently executed and consisted of hundreds of little oscars with
wings. Some of them were blowing trumpets, oblivious

106

to Matthew 6:2. Reverend Hope had been selected as Master of Ceremonies, rather than Reverends Faith and Love, because his name more successfully captured the mood of all the nominees and aspirants who were there. He was, furthermore, an M.E. (Master of Entertainment), a most impressive category in the world of ecclesiastical arts and sciences.

There were five nominees for "Best Achievement in Sound," with the award going to Dr. Sing Song. His acceptance speech was characteristically much too long, though the droning of his words and sentences amply illustrated the fact that he was a worthy recipient of the honor that was bestowed.

The "Best Achievement in Prayer" went to Dr. Flip, whose trousers were perfectly creased. And an oscar for "Best Achievement in Illustration" was awarded to Rev. Inno Vate. In his acceptance speech he thanked his supporting board of elders, the members of which had dressed as various forms of fruit and cavorted in the chancel while he had preached a sermon on Galatians 5:22. He was a double winner because he also received the award for "Best Achievement in Visual Effects." This was for having dressed up as a Bible for the deliverance of his sermon entitled "The Talking Book." The latter was also selected for inclusion in the prestigious *Homiletical Hits,* an annual volume of the year's best messages.

The immense popularity of Dr. Terse was immediately evident by the volume of applause that greeted his appearance. He was given an oscar for "Best Achievement in Short Subjects," having preached a two-and-a-half minute sermon. This topped the previous year's winner, who had been clocked at three minutes even. The "Best Documentary Award" went to Pastor Operator for his slide sermon on "The World's Best Beaches," with the musical background taken from the score of "Let the Lower Lights Be Burning."

"Best Performance by a Clergyman in a Supporting

Role" was won by Ed Minister, who had held up the hands of his senior, a man who needed all the support he could get. "Best Foreign Language Production" was the award captured by Dr. A. Wonder, whose message "The Simple Gospel" had contained 154 quotations from Latin, Greek, Hebrew, and Dutch, interspersed with a few English words, none of which had been less than five syllables in length.

"Best Supporting Performance by a Clergyman's Wife" went to the spouse of Rev. Activist who had spent 365 consecutive evenings alone without going to pieces. "Best Achievement in Costume Design" was a category captured by Rev. Inno Vate, already the possessor of two oscars. It was quite apparent that he was outdistancing the field. His third award was for his appropriate and magnificent attire worn for the delivery of his monologue entitled "I Am Caesar."

And so there were still more awards for still more categories: "Best Achievement in (Bible) Editing," "Production of Best Bulletin," "Production of Best Liturgy," et cetera. All nominees leaned forward to hear their own names called.

Then came the climax—the three biggest awards of all. "Best Performance by a Clergyman"—the winner was U. Dickens Heep for his delivery of the sermon "The First Shall Be Last." "Best Picture of the Year"— the winner was a huge finger painting produced by Rev. Inno Vate's Sunday school class. "Best Easter Extravaganza" (special category) was shared—the winners were Rev. Anne Athema for her development of the theme of "Spring," and Dr. Lucy Fer for the moving sermon, "If Jesus Had Survived His Cross."

What made the event most memorable, however, was what followed the supposed climax of the evening. It was as unexpected as it was unscheduled. From the wings of the stage there strode a stranger in shining garment. He carried a crown instead of an oscar. Inscribed on it were the words "Well Done." The stranger explained that this was an award for the category "Achievement in Faithfulness" and that it was to be given to literally hundreds upon hundreds, none of whom were present.

They were not present because they were "being faithful" in their studies, in their pulpits, visiting the sick, seeking the lost, comforting the sorrowing. And more.

PRAISE THE LORD

We met each other on the sidewalk. Too well acquainted not to break our strides upon meeting, we were, nevertheless, not so familiar with each other as to have anything more than just a brief encounter.

"How are you?" I asked the question absentmindedly because my thoughts were really elsewhere at the moment. When he informed me that he was praising the Lord, my mind focused itself on him more intently. I remembered. He was one of those who always talked that way.

"It's a nice day!" "Is your family well?" "Long time no see!" It seemed he had but one response to every question and observation. He praised the Lord.

His glibness made me restless. Ordinarily one might think that a preacher would be happy to hear such consistent and seemingly devout responses. Instead, they made me increasingly uncomfortable. I felt a growing urge to terminate the conversation. Accordingly, I informed him that I had to be on my way. I had to go to the barber shop.

"I'm going to get a haircut."

His response was no surprise.

"Praise the Lord," he said.

* * *

Easing myself into the barber's chair, I tried to

analyze my feelings about that sidewalk interlude. Why did I feel so negative about it? Was I basically an unspiritual person? Surely "Praise the Lord" was a beautiful expression, urging a still more beautiful activity! The words could be found in many places in the Psalms! Shame on me for negative feelings!

On the other hand, it was possible that there could be some justification for my unenthusiastic attitude. Let's face it. Some people are unbecomingly pious. They attempt to exceed the holiness God requires, let alone live up to it. Christian expressions fall as cliches from their lips, unendingly and thoughtlessly. They sprinkle their language with religious jargon.

I remembered a song of World War II: "Praise the Lord and Pass the Ammunition." I had heard a minister at that time preach a sermon on the third commandment. Predictably, he talked about cursing. In addition, he referred to other forms of vain usage of the Lord's name. Among his illustrations, he mentioned this war song as being contrary to the command to reverence God's name. I remembered agreeing with him. It certainly was a flippant reference to the Deity. But what about such a casual overuse of God's name as I had just heard on my way to a haircut? It seemed so devoutly Christian. And yet—

Closing my eyes to discourage my barber from beginning a conversation, I recalled an incident. I had attended a religious convention some years before. The hotel where I lodged was filled with ministers and missionaries of many denominations, all of them of evangelical stripe.

Hurrying to breakfast one morning, I strode down the long hall to the elevator. Two clerics were already standing at its doors waiting to be transported to a lower level. I could hear their conversation. One was recounting the great things the Lord was doing through his ministry back home. It was taking place in a town not far from my own. The other appeared

111

to be more interested in the elevator than in listening to the information he was receiving. He was anxious for breakfast. Consequently, his rejoinders were more absent-minded than devout. But consider what he was saying!

"Praise the Lord." He repeated the phrase with unction each time his partner gave him an opening.

When I arrived, introductions were in order. After learning my name and church, the hungry one promptly praised the Lord once more. Ordinarily, my heart would have warmed as a result of such fervent thanks expressed for me. If it didn't, it was probably because though he had one eye on me, the other was fastened on the floor indicator. I had the distinct feeling he would like to have seen the elevator rather than me.

My presence elicited a far different response from the other individual. Having claimed a moment before my arrival that the whole state was talking about the Lord's doings through his ministry, and discovering that my town was only fifty miles removed from his, he felt the need of establishing his claim in the mind of Mr. Hungry with my attestation and testimony.

"No doubt you have heard of our great revival," he said. The other man had turned his back completely. He was giving that elevator his full attention. He leaned on the button. He leaned on it again. Meanwhile, I was rummaging through my memory. I could not recall a thing about some great revival in my state.

"I'm sure you've heard of the remarkable results of our month-long campaign."

I had to tell the truth.

"No," I said. "I'm afraid not."

"Praise the Lord," said Mr. Impatient, addressing the closed doors of the elevator in a booming voice.

I do not believe that he had really heard my answer. The man facing me, however, had heard us both. As the elevator finally arrived, he stepped inside, a beaten man before breakfast. I had answered him in the negative. For this his friend had praised the Lord.

"That will be two-fifty." I stepped out of the chair and reached for my wallet. I had the money and a little more besides. How wonderful to be so blessed! A loving family. Good health. Work to do. Food on the table. A wonderful Lord to serve. And enough money for a haircut! It was overwhelming.

As I paid the money and walked out of the shop, I turned to address those who were waiting their turn.

"Praise the Lord," I said. I really meant it.

I hope you do too—every time you use those words.

SUNDAY MORNING

Recently, a newspaper carried a report of an interview it had conducted with a retiring preacher of national renown. In it the man stated that in his entire ministry he had never ascended the pulpit, never initiated a service of worship, without first spending the preceding half hour in quiet meditation and in prayer. Baloney!

I agree that this is the way it ought to be. Consistories that meet prior to services, where elders and deacons sometimes engage in small talk, concluded with prayers that sometimes ramble on and on, are more of a handicap than a help to the man of the cloth facing his hour of truth. Those who are already seated in their pews a full thirty minutes before the time of service have a better opportunity to prepare their hearts for worship, even though they may have come early simply to capture their accustomed pews.

When I was a boy, we rose early on Sunday mornings and stood around the piano for twenty minutes, belting out hymns (favorites: "Jesus, Savior, Pilot Me," "His Eye Is on the Sparrow") to the despair of our good neighbors. After that we went to church, arriving second only to the janitor. There was plenty of time for quiet meditation and prayer or, as in my case, I fear, daydreaming or watching people. Perhaps all this was a bit too much preparation leading up to the main event of Sunday morning. But it was certainly better than those who came running in breathlessly during the singing of the last verse of the first hymn. "Surely," as my father said, "no one would come late for an appointment with the President." It was logical, therefore, to prepare and come in plenty of time for our appointment with Someone higher.

Accordingly, through the years I have always tried to come to church early enough so that, like the preacher in the interview, there would be some time for meditation and prayer in preparation for the service.

But how can the preacher of the interview say that he never varied his habit? Was life that idyllic for him that his pre-service devotions were never interrupted? Didn't he ever have a flat tire, a phone call, or crabby kids? Didn't he ever lose his notes or need a button sewed on, making him late and interrupting his serene routine?

A few weeks ago I faced what I considered to be an unusually taxing morning service. In addition to the regular elements of the order of worship, timing and cimcumstance had contrived to add infant baptism, a brief address by a missionary, reception of new members, Boy Scout recognition, and, immediately following the service, Eagle Scout awards. It promised to be a liturgical mishmash needing a clear head and sure hand at the helm. I went to church, therefore, even earlier than was my custom to make a last-minute check on all things, including myself.

I arrived to find a crisis awaiting me. A couple had been walking the streets all night. She was thinly and briefly clad, bleeding from shoeless feet, with bruised legs and what seemed to be a broken elbow. He was in better condition and only frantic, whereas she was hysterical. As I ushered them into the study, the woman fainted, whereupon the man ran out saying that he couldn't stand such things. I started telephon-

115

ing unsuccessfully for help. Meanwhile, the husband (?) returned, seeking a cigarette which, he said, he needed for his nerves.

When the phone rang, promising assistance, I heard instead the voice of someone asking whether there would be a service, in view of the threatening sky. Hoping that my inquirer would draw no wrong conclusions from the strong female wailing that served as background to my affirmative reply, I looked out and saw the blackest of clouds and sensed the gathering wind. Similar calls were answered with my one foot gently planted on the lady's stomach to keep her prone, remembering a first-aid rule, I thought, that damaged people should not be left to wander.

The clouds burst, creating an instant lake outside. The windows were rattled by thunder and pelted by wind-driven sheets of water. Inside, something went wrong with the organ, and baptism was canceled. It was fifteen minutes to service time with few worshipers in the building, a very large liturgical agenda badly needed last-minute review and probably alterations, and—there was a lady lying on my study floor!

Then, and all in a quarter of an hour, the storm abated. People came. A nurse arrived to help the lady. A deacon appeared to bring the couple to the hospital. The organ cooperated to the extent of being playable. The participants in the service arrived, including the baby to be baptized. Programing the sacrament back into my head and rushing to the pulpit door, I hove into congregational view, hopefully calm in outward appearance, though inwardly harried and shook. There had been no "quiet time" that morning.

By all of which I would make a point. Prepare for church on Sunday morning. If you can, come a little early to quiet your soul and meditate. But if you cannot come a little early, come at least. Sometimes Sunday mornings are not idyllic. The baby won't cooperate. Johnny skins his knee. The dog runs away.

The meat must still be seasoned and deposited in the roaster. Father can't find his tie. So? Life isn't like that preacher in the interview implies. And, God would rather have you rushing in on the last verse of the first hymn than not at all.

THE BABY

Everyone thought Irma Fist was a little funny. She dressed funny. She talked funny. Maybe that was because she had not been in the country very long, having emigrated with her parents from Norway. She also smelled funny! I knew, because she sat right ahead of me in the third grade in the Lutheran school we both attended.

One day during lunch several of us had a big argument. Irma said babies came from their mothers. We all looked at each other as if to say, "Only Irma would say a nutty thing like that." The other kids said they came from a stork. I knew that was wrong too, because I had inside information that babies came from the coal bin. I had looked around in ours, especially after my baby brother was born, and had some questions about it. My doubts, however, did not jar my faith that this was true. Still, I was too timid to set the others straight. I just let them talk.

When the argument grew more heated, all turned to Turk for the final answer. Turk was the biggest, and so his words weighed the most. In fact, Turk drove a Hupmobile to school every morning. He was sixteen years old and in the third grade. Everybody was afraid of him, including me. Sometimes he pricked me with his ink pen when I didn't sit to one side so that he could copy from me when we had tests.

Turk snorted. "Babies," he intoned, "don't come from storks, or mothers, or anything like that." He said they were floated across the Detroit River from Belle Isle (an island between Detroit, Michigan, and Windsor, Canada) in big glass cages. Everybody immediately agreed with Turk. I did too, being afraid to disagree. And so we all made fun of Irma.

Today, third graders don't have arguments anymore. Many are told, for this is a modern age, about birds and bees long before they enter their third year of school.

No, now it's the grown-ups who argue about where babies come from, or, at least, where one baby came from. I mean the baby Jesus. Some say He came like any other baby. Others believe He was "conceived of the Holy Spirit, born of the virgin Mary." These are the ones who say that the Christ Child came down from heaven as the Son of God to save His people from their sins.

I agree with the latter. I hope you do too.

THE BARREL

Tooling down the highway the other evening, I found myself listening to a radio show entitled "Hits of the Forties." Mixed in with the music of Glenn Miller, Benny Goodman, et al., I heard again the familiar but forgotten tones of the Andrews Sisters doing "The Beer Barrel Polka." To be quite frank about it, I found my voice vigorously joining with theirs, even though what they were singing wasn't exactly from the *Psalter Hymnal.*

I remembered listening to them years before while in seminary. While struggling with my nightly Hebrew assignments, their voices emanating from my radio often distracted me with that chorus of "Roll out the barrel."

I say "distracted," for alack and alas, I had no barrel to roll out in those days. I don't mean the type from which one quaffs a brew, but rather the kind that is filled with headier stuff—like sermons.

"Too busy to study this week, Rev.? Why don't you take a couple out of the barrel?" Wherever did that expression come from anyway?

"John has just moved to his second charge. Now he won't have to make any more sermons. All he has to do is turn his barrel upside down." Do people really believe this?

It was true, of course, that in the lean seminary

120

years I had few sermons. Indeed, at the outset I had but one. My text was Luke 22:61, where, after Peter's denial, it says that "the Lord turned, and looked upon Peter." I must have delivered that sermon at least a hundred times. It proved a remarkably adaptable message. I made it fit Christmas, Easter, Advent, and Lent. I used it for Thanksgiving, Pentecost, Fourth of July, Mother's Day, and all the Sundays in between. I presented it to large congregations and small, to churches of various denominations, and at missions where derelicts had to be subjected to it before they could have their bowl of soup. Altogether, I got more mileage out of that sermon than my car, even though the latter was not quite as poorly put together as the former.

Frankly, it was quite a relief to me when I finally doubled the contents of my barrel. With two sermons in my possession I was able to accept invitations for a whole day and not just morning or evening service.

After this there followed a period of time when I grew bolder, accepting requests from places where I had already appeared, making the sermons after setting the dates. This was living dangerously, for what if the muse did not strike before the appointed hour of worship? More than once I submitted sermon titles for bulletins before the sermons themselves were constructed. When this was necessary, the themes were always the same: "The Love of God." For then, as now, I believed that whatever the text, from the Old Testament or New Testament, whichever I would select and whatever I would say, all ought to be able to be subsumed under such a heading.

In my first charge, the contents of my barrel, which was actually a filing cabinet, increased by two sermons each Lord's Day. It was of some concern to me that this cabinet was not fireproof. Not having been able to afford one that embodied this feature, I had to be content with a cheaper variety. But I worried about the possible loss to posterity. I had a dream one night

121

in which, the house in flames, I rescued my barrel first. After that my wife and children.

In my second charge, however, I discovered the limitations of my barrel. Frankly, those old sermons were not all that brilliant. Indeed, upon a rereading, many of them caused me to wonder how I had ever dared to preach them in the first place. Like flowers, many of them had faded. It took more time and effort to breathe new life into them than simply to begin afresh. Many of the illustrations were dated. I also discovered that I had been pretty dogmatic in some questionable areas and that I no longer agreed with some things I had said.

I discovered from other ministers that my experience was not unique. It all argues, therefore, for a measure of restraint to counterbalance whatever urge there had been to rush those deathless (?) homilies into print.

Today, my barrel runneth over. As I look at the files upon files of sermons I have produced, I often ask myself two questions: How can one limited person produce so many? And second, how can one insignificant person presume to say so much?

The answer to the first question is: One at a time. It is good that the Lord does not require that we fulfill our life's assignments all at once.

The answer to the second question is: The love of God in Christ. It is so inexhaustible that, in a day in which sermons are downgraded, we ought to produce even more, not less, filling a barrel so big that I suppose (to paraphrase John 21:25) the world itself could not contain the sermons that should be written.

THE CAPTAIN OF THE AZOLLA

Stanley White, my best friend, was almost seven-and-one-half years old and sort of Roman Catholic. I was a few months younger and definitely, without question, Christian Reformed—facts which meant that he could lord it over me in all things, by reason of age, except religion. That's why I refused to go with him into the corner candy store that Sunday afternoon long years ago. But when he emerged a few moments later, I was not strong enough to resist the licorice stick with which he tempted me. That evening in church the minister looked straight in my direction. Of course. With one look, he turned my guilty conscience into a stomach ache. It was a good lesson for me to remember. Candy purchased on the Lord's Day will make you sick!

"Enlightened" readers who wish to commiserate may hold their sympathy. Those Sundays of long ago were wonderful. Father was home; my favorite toy, an electric train, could be brought out of the closet on no other day; the meal was the best of the week; and all those Sunday clothes gave the day a festive air. Of course, church attendance was mandatory. Twice. Also, there were things you could not do—like listen to the radio or go "joy-riding" in the family car. Yet these strictures, rather than detracting, somehow added to the dimension of the day.

This is not to say that there were not real sacrifices to be made. For example, I had to put out of my mind any thought of ever becoming Charlie Gehringer's successor as second baseman for the Detroit Tigers. This was, indeed, a burden. I had a friend in catechism class who was equally sad because of similar yearnings he thought would be forever unfulfilled. I recall a twitch of envy when, sometime later, it was suddenly all right for him to go to Sunday games because he had turned Lutheran. Yet, all in all, those Sundays, including those repeated countings of the organ pipes in church when my mind wandered from the sermons, constituted a real head start for me. I would not trade them for anything.

It follows from this that I view today's growing permissiveness in respect to Sabbath observance with some thoughtfulness. Far be it from me to impose such a regimen as I witnessed on a preaching engagement one weekend when the children of my hosts could only sing hymns, read the Sunday school papers, or take a walk around the block. I couldn't blame them for labeling Sunday—day of all the week the worst. But the pendulum can swing too far in the other direction too.

There is something healthy in our learning that man was not made for the Sabbath (Mark 2:27). At the same time, however, we must remember that the Sabbath was not made for stadium turnstiles, lying abed, endless homework, and evening TV services conducted by comedians. Those who think it is do well to listen, if not to me, to Captain DeWit.

I met him in Germany, in Koblenz. It was Sunday, and there was an evangelical church a few blocks from the hotel. Upon entering the church, I overheard some ladies talking to one another in Dutch. After the service I spoke to them and suddenly found myself surrounded by thirty people who were delighted to hear an American speaking to them in their native tongue.

Then their leader appeared, a young man in his mid-twenties and handsome enough to be straight out of Hollywood.

He was captain of the *Azolla*, out of Rotterdam, a pleasure craft that plied the Rhine. Before we departed, he extended an invitation to come aboard the ship that evening for a cup of coffee. When we did, and found a hundred or more passengers aboard, I expressed my delight in discovering that he was of the same faith as my own and that we had met in church that morning.

"I never miss," he said, "and I always take as many passengers with me as will come."

"Tremendous," I thought. But what he added was even better.

Looking out over the river, warm and still in the evening air, he said, "I sail these waters all summer long, but when it's Sunday, wherever I am, that's where I drop my anchor."

"I must write about this man one day," I thought, "mentioning both his name and his ship. He deserves a free commercial."

THE CHERRY TREE

When I was a child I spake as a child and said that I would move heaven and earth to own a rabbit. Soon thereafter, having obtained one, and having tired of the responsibility, I strove mightily to be rid of it.

When I was an adolescent I spake as an adolescent and said that what I wanted more than anything in the world was the Ford down the street that was for sale. After buying it, nothing mattered—a dozen repair bills later—but to be utterly and completely rid of it forever.

Now that I am a man I have not put aside my childish and adolescent ways. I could never understand why little George Washington demolished a cherry tree. Today I comprehend his act completely.

I had always been fond of what crossword puzzles unfailingly refer to as large woody plants. Cherry trees were especially dear to me. Accordingly, a dozen years ago or so, I asked that I be given one for Father's Day. The wish being granted, I settled snugly in my easy chair by the window to observe its growth and to dream of days to come wherein I would saunter out of doors to pluck my favorite fruit at will: juicy, red, and all my very own.

The waiting took more patience than I had planned to give. Meanwhile, worrisome little tumors began to grow, discoloration and oozing sap became evident, some blight appeared affecting leaves, and a million nasty bugs moved in, dropping themselves on me whenever I drew near. I had always assumed that trees grew unattended, like Topsys, but this one was turning out to be more labor than it was worth.

A tree surgeon had to be consulted. A spray was prescribed. But the wind always put most of it on me. Whenever this happened, my wife, being completely dedicated to my health and well-being, forced me to take showers, shampoos, and change my clothing, meanwhile interrogating me on whether or not I had inhaled any of the poison I had sprayed. As I said, it was all a lot of bother, leading to some second thoughts.

Everything seemed worthwhile, however, when the first fruits finally appeared, pale pink and basking in the sun. But I had been patient far too long to await their ripening. I discovered during the following sleepless night that consuming several dozen cherries prematurely could upset more than just one's appetite.

It was another negative experience. Yet even when added to all the others, nothing compared to the distresses and frustrations that lay ahead. The following year the fruit appeared in unbelievable abundance, promising a bumper harvest. It also produced a new chemistry in the neighborhood whereby I began to look suspiciously upon all small children as potential cherry thieves.

It was a cloud of birds, however, that plucked my tree as bare as the basket in the dream of Pharaoh's baker. Those winged creatures, straight out of Hitchcock's horror movie, garnered where I had labored and reaped where I had sown. I was so full of indignation I could have screamed "fudge and fiddlesticks" had I not been a preacher. The thought that all my working and waiting had been for the birds was more than I could bear.

The following spring I purchased, at considerable

expense, a kind of net. Made of spun glass, it was difficult to place, itchy to the skin, and an abomination to the eyes. Studying my sermons on Sunday afternoons, I found it distracting to see the many cars slowing and pausing before the parsonage to inspect what appeared to be a giant fungus completely enveloping the preacher's tree. It is true that my purchase inhibited the birds. But it did the same for the cherries. They simply would not grow, while for the rest of the summer, ugly strands of glass hair clung to the branches like Spanish moss in a Georgia forest.

The following summer was equally provoking. Called to serve my denomination as a delegate to synod, I grumbled about church fathers scheduling our highest assemblage at cherry-picking time. It was hard for me to sink my teeth into matters theological, knowing that at the same time beaks were digging into my fruit. Synod and my cherries were finished at about the same time that year.

It seemed to some that these birds were driving me out of my tree in more ways than one. The following year my neighbors were sure of it. I studied under it and in it, came charging out of the house at all hours, in an effort to intimidate grackles, robins, sparrows, and other robbers of the sky. I purchased forty dollars' worth of cheesecloth to make a kind of tree suit, but it didn't fit, and I couldn't get my tree to wear it in the wind. Anyway, it looked indecent. Meanwhile, the birds came for their annual convention, for which I was again their unwilling caterer.

*   *   *

There was a time when I wanted nothing so much as a rabbit, a car, and a cherry tree. There was a time when I wanted nothing so much as to get rid of a rabbit and a car. Presently, there is nothing I want to unload so much as that large woody plant behind the house. For one thing, I'm going to synod again, where, for the same reason as before, I'll find it hard to concentrate.

Like little George, I have a hatchet. Yet while fingering it yesterday, I didn't think of my tree. Instead, oddly, I thought of the experience of Jesus Christ.

He wanted, more than anything, a church on earth. He was willing to suffer to obtain it. But now that it is His, it gives Him so much grief and trouble—more, it seems, than it is worth. How great, then, that, unlike a boy with a rabbit, an adolescent with a car, or a preacher with a cherry tree, He wouldn't think of getting rid of it.

THE GOSPEL UNDER WRAPS

Have you ever heard of "Packaging Engineers"? There is a building on the campus of Michigan State University where they presumably train such people. Its sign simply reads, "Package Engineering," and someday I'm going to enter and investigate the rooms. No doubt it is a perfectly respectable place where, in this fast-moving age, a new science, unheard of when I was a boy, is being taught, mastered, and developed. Who knows! With the population explosion, this department of the modern university may yet prove more beneficial to mankind than all the courses in philosophy combined, as its graduates, experts in the utilization of space, neatly arrange like sardines in a can the billions upon billions of human bodies throughout the world of the future.

In my present mood, however, I am more inclined to consider these engineers as humanity's tormentors—not benefactors. Take the other day for example. I took a shower. Soaking wet, I reached for a newly purchased plastic container of shampoo, unscrewed the top, held the whole thing over my head, and squeezed. Nothing!

I had forgotten, you see, to perforate the opening. But where in the world was I supposed to find a pin, or its equivalent, while standing in the shower!? I was certainly in no condition, furthermore, to look for one.

All I could do was stand there, manfully striving to keep my pastoral cool over some dumb packaging engineer who was responsible for my plight.

Or, take a loaf of bread. My wife wants me to open the wrapper carefully—and I try. But it's not possible. I always end up tearing it, just like the box of breakfast food. Then there are those mustard and ketchup containers in restaurants. All you have to do, according to the instructions, is rip them along the little red line. Hah! And how about those tubes of braunschweiger or liver sausage? A person could starve to death trying to get them open if he didn't go to the sewing box for a pair of scissors.

The other day I received a package of books in a cardboard box. The books are on my desk—finally. But I have broken fingernails. And so in the shower, at the kitchen table, in restaurants, or while trying to get through all those wires enclosing a box containing this year's supply of the *Acts of Synod* for consistory members, I sometimes make little remarks under my breath about packaging engineers.

It may be, however, that the best (?) package engineering is taught, perfected, and practiced, not in buildings on campuses designated for this science, but in some churches and by some Christians who have the Savior so wrapped up that no soul can get to Him. Could it be that there are people who starve to death simply because we have made the Bread of Life so inaccessible?

I recall the story of the black man who went to a certain "white" church one Sunday morning. Apparently it was a congregation which believed in the segregation of the races. Instead of being shown a seat, he was ushered out. On the sidewalk he met Jesus Christ, who said, "Don't feel too badly, please. You've only tried it once. I've tried to get into that church for years, and I haven't made it yet."

And so it is. There are some churches where Christ

131

cannot get in. The more's the pity. But there are other churches where Christ can't get out because He's so boxed and packaged.

I am reminded of the first riddle I ever heard in my life. It was in Sunday school. Said an older scholar in a whisper during the superintendent's prayer, "I'm in a church, see, and it has no doors and windows. How do I get out?" Answer: "It's a holy (hole-ly) church." I didn't get the point. I had not yet been introduced to puns. Now that I do understand this bit of junior humor, I wish more of our churches were "hole-ly" so that our Lord would not be confined within the walls we've built.

I have the same wish for all of us as individuals. "Christ in you" doesn't mean that He must be a prisoner there. To say, "Perhaps we do not testify as readily as some other Christians, but the faith inside us is deep and real and solid," is to forget that our Master did not say we were His packages, but rather, His witnesses.

In the Sermon on the Mount, He had more to say on this whole matter of package engineering. He said, "Don't hide your light under a bushel."

I tried that once. I thought the bushel would burn. Instead, the light went out.

THE HOSPITAL BED

Many people have told me about their operations. Sometimes in considerable detail. I shall resist the urge to tell you about mine.

Instead, let me say a word about the hospital bed, an article which modern designers and engineers have refined to a marvelous motorized piece of perfection.

A hospital bed is a thing apart. I have stood beside many of them while making my pastoral rounds. But on all of these occasions I have never really understood what it was to lie in one. Now that I have been an occupant myself, I am persuaded that every seminary student should be required to go and do likewise, even though he may be in perfect health. For a hospital bed is a vantage point presenting new perspectives.

A hospital bed is a launching pad into another world, observed and contemplated only by patients. A hospital bed is a lonely island, even though it is completely devoid of privacy. It may rest the bones, but not the heart, rendering the spirit apprehensive. Going to the hospital to occupy such an object a few years ago, it came as a shock to me when the nurse told me to undress, climb up, and get in.

My first sensation was one of novelty. It was fun to manipulate the levers adjusting the head and foot ends to different heights and levels. But one can occupy himself in this manner for only so long. It is a novelty which soon wears itself thin.

My next sensation was that my hospital bed was a shelf and that I was on it. Outside the window I could see automobiles carrying occupants to their appointed rounds and tasks, while the hallways echoed with the sounds of hurrying feet. Mine, however, were idle. Contemplating them brought the disquieting realization that the world was going on without me and that it seemed to be doing this very well. I was sidetracked. I had often pontificated that we are all expendable. To say the least, it was something less than reassuring to discover that I was no exception.

An intern came to take my history. I was happy to tell him something about myself. I warmed to my subject. But he seemed not at all interested in my educational attainments or professional progress. Instead, he wanted information about various parts of my body, which made me feel like I was an object. A thing. Surely I was more than the sum of all my physical parts.

A minister came. As a boy I used to wonder who was my barber's barber. Or didn't he have one? On the way to the hospital, I had a similar question: Who is the pastor's pastor? The one who came prayed with me. So did an elder. I had functioned similarly countless times. Now I was on the receiving end and, thereby, made another discovery. I found that it was easier to pray for someone else than to have someone else pray for me. It was not only more blessed, but, in this case, easier to give than to receive. Lying prone on a bed with someone standing over me in prayer was, though moving, a sobering experience.

After family and friends had left, my hospital bed turned into something else—a place of such thorough self-examination as no intern could administer. What if something went wrong! Was I, indeed, ready to meet my Maker? My bed became a wrestling pad. Was I ready to give up my loved ones, my work, and my whole world? Too bad that such introspection is so largely confined to hospital beds. Yet how comfortable a hospital bed can become when relaxing in it finally— not with a sleeping pill, but with the words, "Thy will be done."

It all added up to a valuable lesson. A hospital bed is always a place of profit for the Christian. Sometimes physically. But always spiritually.

To those presently occupying beds of pain more severe than my own turned out to be, I say, not lightly, that there is truth in Psalm 119:71.

To all those who contemplate a trip to the hospital in the future, I say, also not lightly, that God works all things, even hospital beds, for good, for those who are His children.

THE ORDINATION OF A BISHOP

Some time ago I received an invitation to attend the ceremony of ordination for a Roman Catholic bishop. It was to be held in St. Andrew's Cathedral, a few blocks from my church. In the spirit of Vatican II, a number of the Protestant clergy were invited. The affair was to take place September 26, which, unknown to me all these years, is the day of the feast of the North American Martyrs.

The invitation was beautifully inscribed, the language formal and a little strange to my non-Catholic eyes. It read in part: "The Right Reverend, Very Reverend, and Reverend Clergy will vest in the Cafeteria of the Cathedral." I was sure this notification contained a misprint. On second thought, I decided, this could not be so. After all, why should the Reverend Clergy rest in the cafeteria?

My initial reaction to the invitation was negative. Having stated publicly on a few occasions that if everybody in the world turned Roman Catholic, I would be the last; feeling the glances of my forefathers over my shoulders, some of whom suffered religious persecution by way of the Spanish Inquisition; and what with plenty of other things to do, I decided I could observe the feast of the North American Martyrs more profitably some other way.

These inclinations, however, were counterbalanced

by other considerations. Here was a gesture on the part of the local church of Rome. Ought it to be rebuffed? Here was an opportunity, by favorable response, to encourage more lines of communication in these fractured days. Ought they to be discouraged? Furthermore, what would most truly reflect the real spirit of the Reformation and its Lord in these days of deformation?

When I arrived, I noticed that among other displaced clergy there were a few of my own denomination. It gave me a warm feeling. Soon thereafter (having indeed vested in the cafeteria), a procession began that eventually deposited us in our places in the sanctuary. This procedure was accompanied by a thousand voices singing "The Church's one foundation is Jesus Christ her Lord"—an experience that produced in me an even warmer feeling.

In my late teens I had served as organist for the afternoon Dutch services in my home church. As a consequence, I learned and came to love all those Psalm tunes my father and others could sing so lustily. Imagine, then, what a heart-skipping experience it was to hear the rafters of St. Andrew's Cathedral ring with the music of one of those melodies from the Genevan Psalter, used by our generations for the singing of Psalms 66, 98, and 118!

But if I was moved, so—as one priest told me later—were he and all the others present who were followers of His Holiness, Pope Paul VI. "Did you notice it was all in English?" he asked. "Never before have they had so much congregational participation," he added. And his eyes shone and were a little moist.

True, there were some other features of the ceremony that shook me in the opposite direction. The Litany of the Saints with the response of the people, "Pray for us," sung in endless refrain brought particular adverse reaction to my Protestant soul. The pageantry, symbolism, and liturgical complexities were more horizontal than vertical in their sum total effects —not only on me, but also, as I noticed, on many others of the flock of Rome who were more watchers than worshipers. Reflection afterward produced conclusions, some frivolous and others more profound. Among them:

—Roman Catholics and Protestants will never formally unite, as is the hope of some. It is impossible. Rome's view of the church was the foundation for every aspect of the ceremony witnessed and is too much a part of her very warp and woof to allow for any adjustments in a Protestant direction.

—Accentuating the positive, Rome and conservative Protestants are going to move closer together in the years ahead. It is happening now. Belief in the divinity of Jesus Christ is a tie that binds, making such children of the Reformation as myself to feel more comfortable in St. Andrew's Cathedral than in such Protestant edifices where our Lord's true nature is denied.

—Our uninspiring form for the ordination or installation of ministers of the Word is at least shorter than its Roman counterpart. After more than two hours of ritual, I found it indeed necessary to rest—not vest—in the cafeteria.

THE PRIZE

If any member of the church I serve should walk away from some future Sunday service declaring that the preacher is full of beans, he will probably be speaking the truth.

You see, I have a garden. Last season it amounted to a hill of beans. This year it seems more like a mountain. We eat beans. We freeze beans. We give beans away. But still they keep coming. When they do, they demand immediate attention. They must be picked, snipped, snapped, washed, blanched, packaged, and frozen in a hurry. If this is not done, they refuse to be tender and insist on being tough—which is unreasonable.

Accordingly, I had to hie myself off to the garden again the other day to pluck another bagful of my luscious blessings, despite the fact that I really had other things to do. Taking them home with me with the intention of dumping them on my weary helpmeet, I suddenly remembered that my wife had left me. Temporarily.

She was gone for the day. Thinking it unkind and, perhaps, unwise to have her discover at the end of the day more of my garden product in her kitchen, I set myself the task of snipping and snapping, seeking to relieve the tedium by performing this exercise in front of the TV set. It was in this manner that I discovered the wonders of daytime television—something I had forgotten existed.

It was a giveaway show, interspersed with much advertising. Then another and still another show, with prizes that were simply overwhelming. As I am presently saving towards the purchase of a new automobile, I sat there struggling to keep the tenth commandment while I witnessed two contestants on different shows walk off with the keys to brand-new means of transportation. Cars, that is.

I recalled the bygone days of radio when a whole nation tingled to a rash and lavish program called "The Sixty-Four Dollar Question." Answering a simple query, a person could win two dollars, doubling the amount by a second correct answer, and so on, all the way up to an astonishing sixty-four dollars. A man could quit anytime he wished. But most people, having worked themselves up to thirty-two dollars, elected recklessly to go all the way—to cries from the audience of "You'll be sorry!" Those who were successful went home with sixty-four whole dollar bills! Imagine!

With the onset of television and affluence, the above-named sum became piddling. Now people strove for sixty-four thousand dollar prizes, and even more.

These were my thoughts as I sat there snipping and snapping and watching. As some new contestant suddenly became richer by one refrigerator, one sewing machine, one television set, and two tickets to some Broadway show, I recalled a year in seminary when I was so financially embarrassed that I took a whole evening off from Hebrew to complete, in twenty-five words or less, the sentence, "I like Ivory Soap because. . . ." I sent in a dozen entries with a dozen box-tops. I was sure I would win the five hundred dollars I needed so desperately, but I never received an answer. I also made as many words as I could think of out of the name "Finsterwald Furniture." This time I was slightly more successful in that I won a ten dollar credit towards the purchase of a living room suite—an item I needed something less than desperately. As it turned out, everyone else who entered that same contest received the same certificate.

Snip. Snap. A lady was squealing her delight, having just won a weekend in Hawaii for two. How come I never won anything? I thought of all those *Reader's Digest* and Longine Symphonette contests I had entered. "If you do not take advantage of our wonderful offer, you are still eligible to win the grand prize. Just enclose your answer in the 'yes' or 'no' envelope." These letters were addressed to me personally! What a dilemma! If I should win, how would I ever exercise my option? Would I take the house and thirty-six hundred dollars cash, or the house and one hundred dollars a month for life? While working on this problem and my beans, another housewife swooned, having just won an ermine coat for singing "Twinkle, Twinkle Little Star" correctly. Finishing the beans, I took off for a round of calls.

The traffic was light. Tooling down the road, I began to conjure up a giveaway show to end all giveaway shows. The prize would be much more than sixty-four dollars, or even sixty-four thousand dollars. It would amount to more than all the refrigerators and ermine coats and travel tickets and cars in existence anywhere, all to be won by simply answering correctly one single question. I began to imagine the scene.

I was the emcee. I showed my contestant a picture of the prize. The whole world and every country in it, with everything each contained, plus the stars in space above. I asked her if she was ready. A hush fell over the studio audience and two-hundred million viewers. Not one soul breathed all across the land as I opened the envelope and read slowly and distinctly.

What a pity! What a great pity! She tried her

hardest, played for time, and racked her brain. But, alas, though she answered, she answered incorrectly.

The question? It was the first of many, which, with their answers, constitute the contents of the Heidelberg Catechism.

What is your only comfort in life and death?

As I said—what a pity!

Arriving at my destination, I reconsidered what my imagination had brought to mind, rejecting my idea as one which might convey a false impression. After all, Christianity's emphasis is not on getting, but on giving. All the same, I thought, "all things are yours; whether Paul, or Apollos, or Cephas, or the world, or life, or death, or things present, or things to come"—if you are Christ's (1 Cor. 3:21-23).

And they are mine. Because I am his, the world is mine.

Beans and all.

THE RESTLESS ONES

We travel on the earth's axis, from dawn to dawn, at the rate of a thousand miles an hour. At the same time, and together with Mars, Saturn, Jupiter, and Neptune, we travel around the sun at the rate of a thousand miles a minute. And while all of this is going on, we are also hurtling as a universe, including the sun, in a third direction at who knows what speed. Yet despite all of this activity, we are still eternally wanting to go somewhere! Many of our ancestors lived their whole lives in one village, never leaving its environs. But we are the restless ones.

Accordingly, we go south in winter, north in summer, and east or west whenever we have the opportunity. Children are made to sit still in church by parents who seldom sit still in life. Perhaps no previous generation has been to so many places, including the moon, as this present one. Yet at the same time, perhaps, no generation has seen less. To paraphrase Winston Churchill: never have so many gone so far and seen so little! Robert Paul Smith wrote a book some years ago entitled *Where Did You Go? Out. What Did You Do? Nothing.* So, too, some of us might entitle our autobiographies *Where Did You Go? Everywhere. What Did You See? Not Much.* Pussy Cat traveled long and far to London town, yet never saw the Queen. But many human beings travel around

143

the world and never see the King—or any of His handi-work. To borrow a thought from a movie title, some people on travel tours know where they are only by consulting their itineraries. "Today is Tuesday—this must be Belgium."

I have a friend who recently took a course in botany. Together with the other members of his class, he had to stake out an area of ground one yard square and then list everything he could find within his little piece of territory. He was amazed at how much he found. But when he finished, he was even more amazed at how many items the teacher pointed out that he had missed. I have a similar experience when, occasionally, I walk the five miles I usually ride. I am surprised that there is so much under my nose I did not know existed because I never took the time to look. All of which, when applied to life, makes me feel uncomfortable.

I am reminded of *Our Town*, a play by Thornton Wilder. In it a young girl dies. In the after-life she is granted her wish to see the reenactment of a day of her life on earth. As she watches, she calls to her parents to stop doing what they are doing and just look at their daughter instead. "You won't have her much longer," she calls. But busyness keeps them from spending time with a dear girl they will soon never see again. So it is with us. While running, instead of walking, the road of life, we see so little of the scenery and so little of each other.

Seeing so little of the scenery reminds me of the lady and the train. Mrs. "Traveler-through-this-world" took altogether too much luggage for her short trip. The porter helped her get settled, wishing her a pleasant journey, and told her that she would reach her destination—a town called "End-of-the-line"—in record time.

She did. But before she did, consider what took place. As soon as the train started, the lady felt a draft. She changed seats. But on the other side of the aisle the sun came in much too brightly, and so she changed her seat again. This time she located too close to a mother with a noisy child. Again she sought another place. But it, too, proved as unsatisfactory as the others. It seemed to be over the heating unit or something. At any rate, it was much too hot.

Again she found another place—an ideal one. But by this time she was much too exhausted to enjoy it. Furthermore, no sooner had she settled herself when the conductor came to announce that they were at "End-of-the-line." He smiled at her and asked whether she had enjoyed the beautiful countryside through which they had traveled. What a shame that she had seen none of it. She could have done with a little of Philippians 4:11.

It is hoped that soon some of us will settle down, read a book, and spend some time with the family. Once upon a time there was a man who was so "busy here and there" (1 Kings 20:40) that he let his prisoner escape. Too many of us are his children. In being "busy here and there," it is life itself we lose.

THE SACRIFICE

A few years ago I had the privilege of spending some time in Cambridge, England. While there I met many interesting people, not the least of whom was a man who held a minor position in one of the local banking establishments. Occasionally we drank tea together.

During one of our casual visits he informed me that he had been a pilot during World War II. Once while on a routine mission he was forced, because of mechanical failures, to make an emergency landing in Holland. When on the ground, he destroyed his aircraft and sought cover. Almost immediately thereafter he found himself in the hands of six Dutchmen who, through underground connections, were able to set such wheels in motion as eventuated in his return to what in those days was not so merrie-old-England.

It was a hairy tale, told with characteristic English understatement. I listened with admiration, not only for him, but for his saviors. Being of Dutch descent, I felt my kinship with his rescuers and thought that, but for their daring and bravery, the man with whom I was drinking tea might not even be alive to tell his story to a visiting American.

*   *   *

A few weeks ago I found myself fascinated by a

book entitled *Hurrah for Life,* written in the Dutch language by Rev. J. J. Buskes, a retired clergyman. It is a hefty paperback in the nature of an autobiography. I thought it was most heartening that a minister emeritus could go through a half-century as preacher and pastor, experience the rigors of two world wars and several more ecclesiastical battles, and still come up with a book bearing such an optimistic title.

Many of his observations are stimulating and sufficiently thought-provoking to merit attention in these few lines of writing. Their inclusion, however, would only make for digression. What I wish to emphasize solely is that three-quarters of the way through my reading of Buskes, I was suddenly and forcefully reminded of my English tea-drinking, banking, World War II pilot friend who had almost slipped out of my memory.

In a chapter entitled "War Memories," the author of *Hurrah for Life* recalled a time when he had been apprehended and imprisoned for the propagation of such views as were contrary to those of the occupying power. Late one evening the peace and quiet of his cell was interrupted. Eight men were being placed behind bars. They had apparently given aid and comfort to a grounded British flyer, for which crime three of them had received a life sentence, with the remaining five condemned to death by firing squad.

The sympathetic jailer offered, after the authorities had disappeared, to look the other way while the minister visited each one, and he left the clergyman's cell door unlocked to make this possible. The oldest of the five condemned men was sixty, while the youngest was twenty-two. All were from church backgrounds, though none of them had attended a church service for years. As matters developed, their executions were delayed a few days, during which time Rev. Buskes was used of the Lord for all of them.

The oldest of the prisoners acknowledged that he

147

had ignored God's knockings at his door for most of his adult life. But now he came to his Maker's door and found it open.

The roughest of the five at first refused to pray with the minister. Yet just before he was summoned to his execution, he said that though he would not bow his head before the Germans when they stood him against the wall, he had bowed his head to God.

The youngest, executed on his birthday, wrote in a last note to his parents that they should, by all means, read the closing verses of Romans 8.

❋   ❋   ❋

Reading the story of these five men moved me deeply. I wondered: Could it be that they had all sacrificed their lives for that particular Englishman with whom I spoke a few years ago?

Probably not. It would be too much of a coincidence. However, one thing is sure: there are a lot of us alive in an eternal sense, and not by coincidence, because of One who sacrificed himself for us two thousand years ago.

THE SIXTH SENSE

In my opinion, all of our five senses are appreciably diminished by the absence of a sixth—the sense of wonder. Without it a man is poor indeed. That's why I want so desperately to hold on to what I have of it and to develop and sharpen it all I can. It isn't easy, for several reasons:

Sophistication—I'm not the world's most traveled individual. Still, I have journeyed a bit. All of which makes me more than the bumpkin who never sees what lies beyond the nearest hill. Having gaped at some marvels in faraway places, I stand in danger, therefore, of yawning at scenes more near at hand. If I don't, credit a neighbor in my first charge, a man twenty years my senior who had spent his entire life in that one community laboring in its largest factory.

Bright-eyed, he invited me one holiday to view some tiresome parade and to be ready early in order to capture his favorite vantage point. Had I known what a lesson I would learn from my unsophisticated friend seated next to me on the curb that day, I would not have dragged my feet as much as I did. He got more out of one lick of an ice cream cone than heads of state nibbling at their caviar, and more out of that parade, complete with the mayor himself, no less, than some people I know who travel around the world. His

149

simplicity stood in refreshing contrast to the jaded tastes of so many of his contemporaries.

Wealth—Like the law of action-reaction in physics, every material gain involves some loss. On a hot summer day I stopped beside a lake to revive myself with a cool glass of root beer, while coveting a boat churning the waters with high speeds and sharp turns. The proprietor of the refreshment stand, a man of unlettered eloquence, following my gaze, furnished me with commentary. "The kid running that boat," he said, "doesn't even weigh ninety pounds. He's twelve years old. It's his birthday and his dad has just given him his present—a twenty-six hundred dollar boat! He'll play with it for a week, then get tired of it and want something else." Drawing me another glass of root beer, he snorted and said, "What this country really needs is another good (?) depression."

I think of this remark sometimes when I look at the picture on my study wall. It is of an old man, seated at a table, giving profound thanks in prayer for a piece of bread and a cup of water.

Age—Nothing is more stupendous to a boy than the sight of an old sailor with an empty sleeve! He stops to stare. Meanwhile, his parents, who by age have become members of the society for the suppression of astonishment, yawn and hurry the lad along. Too bad! I see airplanes in the sky. I used to call them "flying carpets." I haul out my slide projector. I used to call it "the magic lantern." I have grown accustomed to all the miracles of this push-button age. Even astronauts on the moon hardly give me pause. I wonder if Jesus had something of this in mind, too, when He said, "Except you become as a little child."

Familiarity—I am not wild about art galleries. Viewing masterpieces all in a row, my capacity to absorb reaches its limits by the time I come to the fifth canvas. It is better to travel a hundred miles to view one work of art than a multiplicity of them. Familiarity breeds ennui, if not contempt. It is something I must guard against as a minister, dealing daily as I do in the realm of the sacred. It can be the ministry's deepest pitfall.

But what of Bethlehem? *Sophistication* (we've been around), *wealth* (it depletes the spirit of dependency and need), *age* (experience destroys "surprise"), *familiarity* (we can sing December's carols in our sleep): all these conspire to make us view an ancient manger with tired and lackluster eyes. Lots of people join in singing, "O come, let us adore Him, Christ the Lord." But they never come, and they never do adore Him.

Yet surely the Incarnation is the greatest miracle of all. Christmas trees don't thrill me as much as they once did; but that God should come to earth as a little baby should astound me as it did the singing angels fluttering over Judean hills. "And his name shall be called full of wonder" (Isa. 9:6). It will be, if in this modern age there are people who have the Christian sense, the sixth sense—the sense of wonder.

THE SWEEPER: A MODERN PARABLE

My first charge was in Fishagain, the water-wonderland state, in the city of Reborn, hard by metropolitan Introit, made large and famous by Henry Lord the First. I was fresh from seminary and as short on experience as I was long on trepidation. The congregation was kind, however, and most encouraging. But it soon discovered the necessity for showing further graces of patience and understanding, for my faults were numerous and my failures not a few. There were some triumphs too. Not very many, to be truthful. But as one prefers to recount such incidents in life as fall under the latter, rather than the former, heading, even though they may be scarce in number, I shall give you in what follows—and modestly, I trust—an example of one of my early pastoral "successes."

His first name was "Gus" and his last name was "Sunergos." He was Greek by nationality, and though young and healthy, he was discouraged and suffering greatly from lack of motivation. All this he blurted out in the first few minutes of our first interview together, which had been arranged at his request. Further questioning brought forth more facts, some relevant and others not, through all of which I tried to manifest such ministerial deportment as would encourage confidence in me and such further helpful information as might emerge. So it was that he revealed, and I discovered, what his real trouble really was. He hated his job.

He was a sweeper in some broken-down place on West Warring Road. Each day he swept the same floor with the same broom while the minutes dragged and his spirits sagged—for what future was there, and could there ever be, in what he had to do? Was there nothing better? Was there no more to life? The questions seemed rhetorical; not so much addressed to me as to the walls of my small study. For with his head in his hands, he sought no direction—only commiseration.

It was at this point that my mind was struck by Providence. Sympathy would not square his shoulders. Platitudes and cliches would never transform this picture of dejection. Why not, then, I reasoned, urge upon him the most radical course of action of which I could conceive? The shock of it might take his breath away at first. But it might also, if taken seriously, bring new hope and life. Accordingly, I suggested that he go to the largest and most famous and successful concern in all of Reborn, applying for a position to no one less than the owner and operator himself. Henry Lord! To prevent a quick rejoinder in the negative, I kept talking, enlarging on my idea with growing eloquence. "Offer not only your services," I said, "but offer yourself. Tell him that you will give him your all if he will take you into his organization. Big as it is, it's still a growing company," I said, "and being part of it you will have a future and all the motivation in the world."

His reaction was one of incredulity, of course. When he saw that I was serious, he indicated that perhaps I had a problem surpassing his, relating to my sanity. But for all the arguments and objections that he raised, I presented answers and replies. In his last rebuttal to my scheme, he stated that even if he would follow my suggestion, a sweeper, a nobody, would never find entrée with so high a personage as the founder and president of the biggest company going. He'd never even get inside the door, he said. To all of which I replied that Henry Lord was accessible; that I had talked with him many times myself; that I had never found him too busy; that, in fact, I knew of none he'd ever turned away. With that, my visitor took his leave, looking extremely dubious.

During the next few days Gus continued his intolerable existence as before. He went to Warring Road each morning to sweep and feel sorry for himself. But a seed had been planted. A small voice on the inside kept prompting him. "Why not try the minister's idea? What do I have to lose?" So it was that his hesitant feet took him one afternoon to the big administration building of the man I had recommended that he see. What with his shabby dress and halting speech, he fully expected to be repulsed. Imagine his surprise, therefore, when he was told that Henry Lord would see him. Imagine his utter stupefaction when he was further informed that the interview could take place at once.

Precisely what went on behind those closed doors between Lord and Gus I cannot tell, for I was not there to hear. But I do know that when he emerged from that inner office one hour later, he gave the appearance of one quite overcome. For not only had he been offered a job, but a position! Nor was it ordinary, for Gus, with all his lack of skills, had been offered nothing less than a partnership in the firm. It was incredible! It was also true.

The next few weeks were dizzying ones indeed. He was given an office across the hall from that of Henry Lord. In it he found a collection of the company's books and records (somewhere between sixty and seventy of them in number) which he had to peruse and study. He was also given an unlimited expense account. If he had need, he had only to go to the top floor, where, if he would ask, he would receive. So Gus applied himself to mastering the contents of the company's books. At night he loved to walk on Fishagain Avenue, the main street of Reborn, to see the big lighted sign of "Henry Lord Company," which was being changed to read "Henry Lord and Gus Sunergos Company." Thus the young man spent his days while awaiting his special assignment. It was to be given him very soon, so he was told.

And so it happened. He had not even really begun to master those books and records when he received directions as to where to go and what to do. Lord had need of him. He could continue his studies even as he worked. So Gus went to the company bank on the top floor, where he had unlimited resources, but where he asked for only enough to cover bus fare to where he had to go.

All this I learned from Gus who had come to pay me a second visit. He seemed happy and content, a man who had found a purpose and a joy in living. In fact, I hardly recognized him. He was, indeed, a new man.

"But why did you ask only for bus fare," I said, "when you could have asked for more?" I was thinking about that unlimited bank account.

He smiled. "It takes a little time, I suppose, to learn that you can ask for much with confidence."

"But what is your assignment?" I asked somewhat breathlessly, imagining him a director of some outlying plant, with hundreds working under him. As a partner in the biggest company going, I was anxious to know his specific role and task. His answer stunned me into silence.

"I'm a sweeper over on West Warring Road," he said. Seeing that I was speechless, he laughed softly and said, "I know. You have many questions. And I have few answers. I'm doing what I used to do. And yet—it's all so different now. My senior partner has a special interest, apparently, in that floor at the Warring Plant. So, if it's important to him, it's important to me. Doubt me if you will, but believe me if you can. I'm content."

Gus rose to leave. At the door he turned and said, "I have a good Greek name, but I never knew its meaning. Now that I do, it makes a lot of difference." With that, he stepped out into the street.

Later that evening I turned to my Greek lexicon, standard equipment in every pastor's study. "Sunergos," it said, meaning "laborer together with." There was a reference to 1 Corinthians 3:9a. I looked it up. It said, "For we are labourers together with God...."

THE TEN-MINUTE MILE

Many years ago I ran the mile in four minutes flat. This was a great feat, since being but ten years of age at the time, my legs were very short. I had stayed too long, till after dark in fact, at a friend's house reading the *Adventures of Dr. Fu Manchu*. On my way home afterward I imagined great evils lurking in every shadow and between every house, and so ran faster, it seemed, than Jehu (2 Kings 9:20) ever rode.

It wasn't until years later that the four-minute mile was run again, this time by Roger Bannister, track star. That he was acclaimed and I was not lies in the fact that he did it officially. Since Eppinga and Bannister, however, many others have broken the four-minute barrier, all of which brings me to the subject of track meets.

If you have never witnessed track and field events, you have missed one of life's finer experiences. Running, jumping, throwing—here is mankind's oldest sport, begun by Cain and Abel, who, doubtless, raced each other to the nearest tree on more than one occasion. It is true, of course, that football attracts its ten thousands, while track merely draws its tens and hundreds. But I am found among the latter. And while watching, sometimes my heroes are the ones who finish last.

I recall one such person a number of years ago. We

157

never met, nor do I remember his name. A student at a local high school, he ran the mile, or tried at any rate. But he wasn't built for it. His musculature was all wrong and his coordination nonexistent. In comparison with the others, most of whom ran smoothly and with apparent ease, he seemed to be working harder and with less reward. Indeed, it appeared that the god of wind had created air resistance against his blunt frame, for he ran as if into the teeth of a gale with his arms circling like windmills. It was worse than appearing to be on a treadmill, for he seemed almost in danger of losing ground instead of gaining.

When the others came across the finish line, I expected to see some relaxation of effort on his part. On the contrary, he displayed, if anything, an intensification of resolution. With no one watching him, with the officials preparing for the next event, with the winners of "the mile" congratulating one another, Mr. Hopeless was still barreling along on all cylinders with his throttle wide open. When finally he crossed the finish line, entirely unobserved and long forgotten, having run the mile in ten minutes—which seemed more like fifteen—I was on my feet, standing in his honor. For in those ten long minutes he had grown, in my eyes, from the pudgy figure he really was to a giant ten feet tall.

Nor was this all. Imagine my surprise when, a year later, I saw this same young man again in another meet. When the gun went off for the mile run, it was immediately apparent that no improvement over last year's performance could be expected. But the spirit and the heart were there, as grand as the year before. The following season found him present once again, as courageous as he was ponderous, running his long ten-minute mile against hopeless odds: a high school student preaching his powerful sermon for the third time to a lone preacher sitting in the stands.

Watching him, I remembered those Sunday school picnic races of years before in which I was always entered unwillingly because of the presence of one of my classmates whose feet were swifter than my own. Our shoes lay scrambled in a heap at the far end of the field. We had to run, find our footgear, put them on, and race back to the starting line. One year I purchased brand-new tennis shoes so that I could find my own more readily. It was the only race I ever fixed —but lost anyway because one shoe came off just as I was about to finish first. How much better was the spirit of my undaunted, lead-footed, slow-moving hero of the track meet!

However, watching him, I remembered Paul even more than my own earlier character failing. He, too, entered a race once upon a time (2 Tim. 4:7). He started late (Acts 9:18), ran last (1 Cor. 15:9), with a handicap (2 Cor. 12:7); nevertheless, he finished (2 Tim. 4:7) because he wouldn't quit (Phil. 3:14)— and that because he knew, as my hero of the track meet also knew, that winning is not just a matter of swiftness (Eccl. 9:11).

THREE LITTLE WORDS

While in The Netherlands some time ago, I noted that many English words have become part and parcel of the vocabulary of the land. The same thing cannot be said in reverse. Few, if any, Dutch words are in usage in America. However, with citizens of Holland extraction, there are some that are still in circulation. Notably, three. It is likely that even those who have lost all contact with their ancestral tongue are familiar with them. They are: *gezellig, vies,* and *spotten.*

"Gezellig" means companionable, socially convivial, snug and cozy. "Vies" ("v" sounded like "f," rhymes with "niece") can be translated by such words as dirty or filthy. A thing that is "vies" is a thing that is repugnant. "Spotten" ("o" vowel sound approximates Scottish "loch") means to mock or to scoff, particularly regarding matters that are sacred. Time and again I have heard these words fall from the lips of those who do not know another word of Dutch.

The reasons for the survival and durability of this linguistic trinity are at least twofold. First, they are onomatopoetic words—their very sounds conveying their sense. Secondly, as is insisted by many, they are actually untranslatable words. They really have no counterparts in the English language.

The first reason is a solid one. Recently I met a man who hasn't a Dutch bone in his body. Yet in our conversation, he referred to something as being "vies." When I pretended to miss his meaning and asked for an explanation, he said he really couldn't give me a good definition. He had heard it from his friend's mother-in-law, he said, and he liked its sound. What he meant by it, he added, was something akin to "bleah!" The second reason is, I think, equally valid, for time and again in speaking with friends I find myself preferring these three words over their English approximations.

I notice, however, that I am using the first word less, while I have more and more occasion to employ the remaining two. To me this is a significant commentary on our faltering culture. "Gezelligheid" (for those who sense the German language better: "gemutlichkeit") is a fast-fading factor in life in these United States. One reason for my being loath to leave England when I visited it some time ago was that I found a slower pace of living there. It was more "gezellig." Every hour in America seems filled with rush. People scarcely look at one another. Many of our homes are masterpieces of interior decorating, yet not cozy—"gezellig." Our radios and television sets and record players have compulsive twelve-inch speakers stereophonically destroying tranquillity. Our supermarkets, restaurants, and shopping plazas lack soul, while Hallmark cards will deliver such birthday greetings as were formerly conveyed personally. Add, therefore, to the present-day criticisms of our society another, seemingly small yet profound: we are losing the human touch! Even within the communion of the saints "gezelligheid" is losing ground.

The word "vies" comes to my lips twice as much nowadays as the word "gezellig." Presently much in America is unwashed, from people to places to things. There is much to offend the eyes. And nose. The land has B.O. Our rivers stink. Our cities rot. So do our lungs from the air we breathe. A man-made plague of

161

garbage blankets us from shore to shore, while beneath it all, somewhere, lies America the beautiful. If the Dutch prize cleanliness, as is reputed, it is logical that they would come up with a dramatic word for its opposite. Regrettably, there is more occasion for its use today as descriptive not only of our physical, but also moral, climate.

But if I find myself using the word "vies" twice as much as the word "gezellig," I discover I am using the word "spotten" five times more than the other two put together. I remember a film I viewed many years ago: the story and plot are long since forgotten but the title lingers on: *Nothing Sacred*. I find this title eminently descriptive of the mood of so many of my countrymen today. I applaud the present reemphasis on the humanity of Christ. At the same time, I deplore such contemporary presentations of Him in some of our music and drama as deprive Him of His holiness. If He were to walk into my study at this moment, I would kneel. Such a posture, however, is becoming increasingly foreign to our spirit, not only with respect to the Savior, but to so much that formerly was hallowed. If "spotten" means, as it does, to mock or to scoff and scorn those things which ought not to be profaned, then we are doing a lot of it with respect to sex, marriage, honor, church, and the whole Sinaitic code. Some of this is called humor. But it isn't funny. Not long ago someone entered a church and spit derisively into the communion cup. God help him and the astonishing numbers of those who laughed instead of being appalled by such behavior.

Three little words. There is really a fourth, although it is as untranslatable as the other three. It is the word *benauwd* ("tight in the chest," "oppressed," "anxious"). A culture in which there is hardly anything sacred anymore makes me "benauwd" about its future.

TOWARD BETTER VISION

I have begun a new practice lately—I do push-ups and sit-ups while listening to the news on television. It all started some time ago when I bought a new suit. I was shocked to discover that I needed a larger size. When the salesman produced his tape measure, I pulled myself in as best I could. Even so it appeared that I had grown a bit—in the wrong direction.

The meaning of this "development" was reinforced by a card from my eye doctor which arrived in the mail. It gave me a slight shiver as it informed me that my "glasses" were ready and could be picked up any time it was convenient. I dawdled. As a matter of fact, I waited a full two weeks even though it had been possible for me to stop in at the optician's office the very next day.

It wasn't that I was shy of glasses, you must understand, for spectacles have been part of my life for quite a few years. But these were different. These were the dreaded "bifocals," the wearing of which would announce to all my friends that I was getting older, that I was losing my battle with the onslaughts of time. What a miserable moment when I put them on and stood looking at myself in the mirror. Solemnly. Privately.

But who is interested in this minor crisis in my life, only another small concession that I have lately had to make to overtaking age? Suffice it to say that I have swallowed my pride, at least to some degree, and have donned my new glasses publicly, if not as yet regularly. And though I haven't grown accustomed to the fuzzy appearance of my feet on the sidewalk or to arching my neck sufficiently to read the top of the newspaper through the bottom of my glasses, I must admit that there is something to be said for such "specs," through the use of which one can see objects at a distance as well as the small print in those theological tomes that line my shelves. Why, with these on my nose I can see things both near and far away—the distant and the close-at-hand.

It is now my strong conviction that everyone should have bifocals, for the simple reason that everyone needs them. There are people who can see only what is far away, like the grass on the other side of the fence, or the glamour that is Hollywood, or even the world that awaits above. The blessings that are on this side of the fence, the duties that surround, and the needs of this present world are quite out of focus. At the same time there are others, the near-sighted, who see only themselves, their families, and their immediate world of time and things. The needs of their more distant neighbors are, quite literally, out of sight and, therefore, out of mind; while as for the future, it is too far beyond the limits of their vision for them to show concern.

The solution, therefore, is obvious. Bifocals. And the best bifocals in existence are the Holy Scriptures. They are both telescopic and microscopic. My doctor told me that my glasses might make me a little dizzy at first, and even a little sick. The Old and New Testaments are no exception. The vistas they present are dizzying, and the close-ups of the heart can make one ill. But for better vision, there is nothing like the spectacles of God's Word. With the Bible in your hand, if not upon your nose, you can see what you need to see—both near and faraway.

So, don't dawdle. Swallow your pride. Your eyes are not so good. Look through those bifocals the Great Physician has prepared for you. You can pick them up any time it is convenient.

TRAIN OF THOUGHT

At a concert. Rather formal surroundings. The music of a great composer filling the hall, yet not altogether holding my attention. I glanced at the individual seated in my line of vision ahead. He wore blue jeans, sneakers, and a sort of jacket, the open collar of which revealed only an undershirt. "Clothes do not make the man," I thought to myself. "Don't judge a book by its cover. You're reacting like a stuffed shirt." But no matter how hard I tried to ward off all prejudicial thoughts, I could not quite succeed.

I recalled a wedding at which I had officiated sometime earlier when my mind had been engaged in a similar struggle—a ceremony at which the bride and groom had appeared in shirttails. I am not the kind to aspire to anyone's list of the world's ten best-dressed men. Putting my money on my back is not my idea of Christian behavior. I have no admiration for fops or dandies. Still, I could not help thinking of the man in the Bible who lacked the wedding garment. And I couldn't quite squelch the thought that a man who could afford the price of a symphony ticket could surely afford the price of a comb. I guessed I was just a square.

The rich tones of the Brahm's symphony, rising in crescendo, were not strong enough to interrupt my reverie. A pair of brown shoes walked into mental view in the magical darkness of the hall and to the beat of the conductor's baton. They had long since been donated to a local mission. Because I had splurged to possess them, I felt unjustified in replacing them when, shortly after their purchase, I had gone to my new church. There I had to wear a Genevan clerical robe. The ministers who installed me were properly attired: white shirts, black ties, black robes, black shoes. I had stood in their midst, in full view of the congregation: white shirt, black tie, black robe, brown shoes. It had been a moment in which I wished that feet, like hands, could be tucked away into pockets.

I glanced again, as best I could in the darkened hall, at the nonconformist ahead. I pictured him showing up at an ordination in jeans and bare feet, standing unconcerned, unlike myself, amid the dignitaries of the church. I guessed once more that I was just a square.

Watching the kettle drummer softly tuning, I thought he looked a little like George Gobel—one of America's funniest men. I remembered his classic line: "Did you ever imagine that the whole world was a tuxedo and you were a pair of brown shoes?" Sure enough. There had been lots of times when I had not blended in with my surroundings any more than a nonconformist at a concert.

There had been that costume party when I was a lad of twelve, where all the children had been made to dance. I was dressed as a little Dutch boy, complete with wooden shoes. A perfect excuse for not engaging in an activity I considered evil.

"Please dance with those things on."

"No."

"Jump around then."

"No, because that's just the same."

On that occasion I had been the nonconformist, to say nothing of being a bit of a prig.

I recalled my days in a factory, where the talk was

usually filthy and profane. I had been among them, yet not of them. Or, something different: I thought of some inter-church meetings I had been attending. As a Reformed clergyman, I had felt alone. Neither "fundamentalist" nor liberal, neither fish nor fowl.

A play of years ago sprang to mind. A stage full of dancing girls, all costumed alike and wearing identical masks and wigs. A girl had entered from the wings in individual dress. She had stood watching. Gradually, though, she had joined the others and fallen in step. Then a funny thing happened. I never figured out just how. Imperceptibly her dress had changed even as she had danced to coincide with the costumes of all the others. She had also donned an identical mask and wig. Then all the girls had come together in a huddle, and when they fanned out again, the girl from the wings could no longer be identified. The whole thing had brought a text to mind: "Be not conformed to the world."

Better to be a pair of brown shoes, though the whole earth is a tuxedo.

The concert had come to a crashing end. The loud cymbals had brought me back to reality. As I shuffled out into the cold night behind the nonconformist stranger, I still thought that at least he could have used a comb. At the same time, and with apologies to Mr. Brahms, I thanked the man in sneakers, mentally, for a mile long and richly laden train. Of thought.

TRUE STORY??

It was a fine church. It sought to be faithful to God's Word and the confessional standards that were based on God's Word. It had a college and seminary, a radio ministry, and spent great sums of money on home and foreign missions and world relief. But, of course, like every other church, it was not perfect. It had some factionalism in it, some doctrinal disputes, some negligence here and there in the sphere of church discipline, and a few differences in some further areas of Christian life and commitment. Being less than a perfect church, therefore, not a few of its members offered suggestions in their weekly magazine and other places as to how their church could improve and come closer to where it ought to be.

Some said what was needed was more spirituality. What was needed was more prayer meetings. It was their opinion that there was a lack of warmth and emotion, especially in the services of worship. They wanted some "Amens" sung out by the members of the congregation on occasion. They said they wanted more Holy Spirit, some Pentecostal fire, maybe even some speaking in tongues. "That will make us a better church and solve our problems," they said.

Others had a different notion. Equally concerned for the health and well-being of their church, they found the solution in more doctrinal knowledge and understanding. They felt that what was needed was increased and improved catechism classes. They insisted on more theological understanding, more Christian education, more instruction and training in the things of God. "That will make us a better church and solve our problems," they said.

Meanwhile, a third group was of a third opinion. "When all is said and done, what is more important than faith?" they wondered. Surely without faith it is impossible to please God. "Believe on the Lord Jesus Christ and thou shalt be saved, thou and thy house." What was more important than that? In an age of unfaith, wherein many other churches were losing what was once for all delivered unto the saints, it was more trust and confidence in God and His precious promises that was needed. "That will make us a better church and solve all our problems," they said.

But these three points of view, well-articulated and ably defended, not only struggled among themselves for attention, but contended also with a fourth. These people were of the opinion that what was really needed in the church was a much greater spirit of stewardship and self-sacrifice. They decried the fact that so few tithed and gave only meagerly out of their abundance, remembering their obligations to God last —not first. They considered it a shame when they saw so much shining affluence parked in the church lot and so little in the collection plate. What is needed is more of the kind of giving that hurts. "That will make us a better church and solve our problems," they said.

And so there were all these viewpoints. "More fervor!" said the first group. "More knowledge!" cried a second group. "More faith!" said a third. "More sacrifice!" demanded a fourth. And they fell to arguing among themselves. Some even developed hard feelings.

Then a few of the members remembered a letter written to their church by a missionary—sent from across the seas and centuries. It addressed itself precisely to their situation. All four dissenting groups, and others too, gathered together to hear it read, each faction expecting justification in distinction from the others. The missionary, who said he spoke for God—which indeed was true—said that all the groups were right. But, he added, all of them were wrong as well.

Addressing himself to the first group, he said that more warmth was surely needed. "But," he added, "if you have such intense fervor and zeal as will result in speaking in tongues, and have not love, all you will be doing is making noise."

Directing himself to the second group, he said that more knowledge was an absolute must. "But," he added, "if you have so much knowledge as to understand all mysteries, and have not love, it will amount to nothing."

Looking at the third group, he said that more faith was desperately necessary. "But," he added, "if you have as much faith as will remove mountains, and have not love, then faith minus love, like faith minus works, is dead."

Concentrating on the fourth group, he said more sacrifice was, indeed, essential. "But," he added, "if you have such a spirit of sacrifice as not only gives all goods to the poor, but presents your own bodies for burning, and have not love, there is no profit for anyone at all."

And so all four factions, while realizing that increased zeal, knowledge, faith, and sacrifice were all essential, acknowledged that without abiding love they could not be a better church.

And so they became—a better church.

TWO SUITS AND A WHISTLE

There was this unbelievable sale of suits downtown. It had been announced by way of a double-spread ad in the local newspaper. Of course I wasn't going! I wasn't going because if there is anything I dislike more than shopping for a suit, it is shopping for a suit at an unbelievable sale.

Still—where else could I get such a bargain?

My wife, who is somewhat more experienced in these matters, suggested that I arrive early rather than late. Appearing fifteen minutes before the opening hour, I was surprised to find a huge congregation (what other word would a preacher use?) gathered at the door. For some strange reason, my mind made no immediate connection between the presence of so many people and my own. Instead, it occurred to me that some tragedy must have taken place. A fire perhaps. A heart attack. An accident. Inquiring, I was informed by one on the outer edge of this human mass that all in that vast assemblage were present for the same reason I was. I found this piece of intelligence awesome, to say the least.

When, soon thereafter, the doors opened for business, my body fused with all the others into one huge mortal tidal wave whose assault the building somehow survived. Inside, I clung Samson-like to a pillar, though with far less strength. I needed to catch my breath.

Instead, I caught someone else's. A bank president's. Wheezing heavily into my face, he was squeezing by, clutching a sport coat plus an overcoat.

I did a double take. A bank president!

A member of my family, a daughter to be exact, functioned as my aide. She brought three suits, all different colors. She, too, looked strained, like maybe she had just broken the record for swimming the English Channel.

But where should I try them on? The man next to me, in dark glasses, was nonchalantly using the crowded aisle for a dressing room. I refused to emulate his example. I didn't have his legs. More important, I didn't have dark glasses. I found what appeared to be a storage closet. It was private, except for two very attractive mannequins who were just sort of standing there. After turning them to the wall, I proceeded, discovering that the green suit, ridiculously under-priced, fit perfectly.

❊   ❊   ❊

It was a week later. I was sitting at my desk, resplendent in my green one-hundred-dollar suit for which I had paid less than half. Opposite me sat a man, respendent in his brown four-hundred-dollar suit for which he had paid more than twice its price. How so?

Did you ever hear about Franklin's whistle? I do not altogether approve of old Benjamin. Like Solomon, he had too many lady friends. But also like Solomon, he had an uncommon amount of common sense.

One day, as a youngster, he entered a toy shop. Charmed by the sound of a whistle in the possession of another boy, he offered all his money for it. At home, his brothers explained that he had paid four times its worth—a fact which gave young Franklin more chagrin than his whistle gave him pleasure. Ever after, observing the actions of men, he met with many who, in his opinion, were paying too much for their whistle.

He saw some, for example, too ambitious of court favor, sacrificing more than such favor was worth. He observed others, fond of popularity, neglecting duty in their pursuit of acclaim. These, and more, were all paying too much for their whistles.

How true. Remember Ahab and his desire for Naboth's vineyard? The king paid too much for his whistle. Remember Demas who forsook Paul, having loved this present world? Like Ahab, he, too, paid too much for his. But, alas, the world is full of the likes of both.

So is the church.

I have in mind a man who has spent the past decade in the successful pursuit of a career. Many envy him. But I am much worried about his spiritual condition. I fear he has paid too much for his whistle.

I have in mind a couple who can think of nothing but their cottage. Their Sabbath pattern has been broken. I see the effects on the children. They are paying too much for their whistle.

And—I think back to that man in that brown suit facing a pastor clothed in a green bargain. That person sacrificed everything for a life that would include four-hundred-dollar suits—even his marriage, which was then already teetering on the brink. That suit was his whistle. I'm sure he has long since discarded it. But the payments go on and on.

How sad that for every person who gets a bargain, there are ten who pay too much for what they want. That is because they neglect the spiritual Consumer's Report made up of sixty-six books.

I wish that more would lend an ear to those spiritual advisers among us who warn against the purchase of overpriced whistles.

VERSIONS

I am concerned about the ever-increasing number of versions of the Truth.

A few years ago I walked into a catechism class carrying a stack of Bibles the length of my arms, all the way up to my chin. Respectfully depositing them on the desk, one on top of the other, I observed, before the group, that each section of that sacred tower represented a different translation of the Bible.

Inviting comments, I was particularly struck by the remark of one young lady. She thought it quite wonderful that so many people would spend so many hours studying the ancient languages in their efforts toward accuracy in presenting God's Word in English. Suddenly I felt a pang of remorse for so often having studied my Hebrew reluctantly in seminary days. I do not own a hat. But if I did, I would remove it from my head in honor of those who, with talent and patience, pore over ancient manuscripts and conjugations.

It is not their efforts I have in mind when I express concern over the increasing numbers of versions of the Truth. True, their productions are adding to my sermon preparation time. After wrestling with a text in its original form, it was my custom to consult King James and the version "set forth, A.D. 1611, compared with the most ancient authorities and revised A.D. 1881-1885, and newly edited by the American Revision

Committee, A.D., 1901." Now I feel compelled to go further. I must now also consult the *Revised Standard*, the *Berkeley*, the *Amplified*, the *New English, Jerusalem, Phillips*, et cetera, et cetera.

It would be dishonest to say that this is my standard procedure. The fact is that it is a weekly struggle to reserve adequate time for sermon construction. But in my more conscientious moments, I now turn a lot of pages of a lot of Bibles, including *The Living Bible, Good News for Modern Man*, and even one written in my ancestral tongue. It is instructive to note the nuances as they vary from volume to volume.

While I am on this subject, I cannot resist adding the comment that often it is still the King James that gives me the greatest satisfaction. This observation must please those who believe that it only is inspired, and that God, "who spake at sundry times and in diverse manners," always did so in the style of Shakespeare. The truth is that the King James is not always the most accurate. Nor is its style easily grasped by a generation whose language has lost all style.

I simply prefer it for personal reasons. I grew up with it.

To return from this digression, let me reiterate that my concern is not with those increasing numbers of versions, all of which strive for accuracy. It is rather with the increasing numbers of Orwellian versions which rewrite the Truth and which are expressed, if not on paper, in lives that are lived. It has been said that none of the versions is inspired. This is not true. Those that bend or reshape the Truth definitely are inspired—by the devil.

To illustrate such versions of the Truth as give me both pause and pain, allow me to attempt three modern renderings of Psalm 23. The first might well stand as the Communists' version, while the second is presented as the Materialists' translation. When reading the third, please bear in mind that no slur on Christian psychiatrists is intended. It is the version of an alarming number who, despite high learning and modern sophistication, have no understanding of Psalm 8:4,5.

      ❧   ❧   ❧

Karl Marx is my shepherd, I shall not want—eventually. He maketh me to lie. He leadeth me beside the truth. He restoreth all things to the state. He leadeth me in the paths of dialectics for Communism's sake. Yea, though I walk through the valley of the shadow of capitalism, I will not fear; for might is with me. The masses, they comfort me. Thou preparest a table before me laden with what belonged to others. Thou anointest my head with vision and determination. My vodka runneth over. Surely victory and all the world shall follow—eventually, and I will dwell in a Communist state *until I die.*

      ❧   ❧   ❧

Ambition is my shepherd, I shall not want for anything someday. It maketh me not to lie down. It leadeth me to greater effort. It restoreth my energies when I am tired. It leadeth me into such paths as will further and hurry my progress. Yea, though I walk through the valley of the shadow of reversal, I will not fear, but press on relentlessly, for the future is with me. The goal, the prize, success—they dazzle me. Thou preparest a table before me in a big mansion someday. Thou anointest my head with great determination; the possibilities run over. Surely wealth and position will be my lot for the rest of my days, and I will dwell in the gates of the city, honored and admired, *until I die.*

      ❧   ❧   ❧

My psychiatrist is my shepherd, I shall not worry. He maketh me to lie down upon his couch. He leadeth me beside supportive, non-directive waters. He restoreth my Id. He leadeth me into client-centered therapy for my Ego's sake. Yet, though I walk through

177

scopophilic valleys and erogenous zones, I will fear no sin. For Freud is with me. His libido comforteth me. He prepareth pleasure centers in the presence of my retroactive inhibitions. He anointeth my Superego with sublimating conditioners. My self-realization runneth over. Surely reinforcements and appointments with my psychiatrist shall follow me all the days of my life, and I shall dwell in the presence of Aha Phenomena *until I die.*

WHAT HAS GOD WROUGHT?

"Today marks the sixth anniversary of my return to sobriety. What hath God wrought! B.R."

A year later I had received a similar message except that "sixth" was changed to "seventh." Rummaging through some old files a few weeks ago, I came upon these grateful words penned over twenty years ago.

As a young man of unusual promise, B.R. had gone too far too fast. Successful in business and in politics, there seemed to be no limit to his future. But along with success, the bottle, too, went to his head. And body. Gradually his ascending star began to level off—plummeting finally and precipitously.

It was the old, old story—but not the one Christians sing about in church. He lost his business and his family. Equally tragic was the fact that he did not lose an unwarranted pride and confidence in himself. He became a lush—yet one who could quit the habit anytime he wanted.

Or so he said.

Floating on alcohol, he drifted away into the mouth of metropolis, which swallowed him whole. There he filled his belly with beverage even swine wouldn't touch. For almost a score of years he lived in a fog which the brightest noonday sun could never penetrate. It was difficult to imagine that once upon a time he had been a fine young man standing up in a Sunday morning service making a profession of his faith.

He began to beg and grow expert in all those clumsy skills necessary for the support of unholy thirst. He lied when it was necessary, and soon discovered that he was also lying when it was not necessary. Sometimes he borrowed, swearing on a stack of Bibles that he would repay the following day. But even as he swore, he had no intention whatsoever of returning the dime or dollar he would melt into booze and absorb into his pores.

He had seen dead bodies in doorways on skid row. It was the only sight that gave him pause. Accordingly, when he fell gravely ill, or so he thought, he hitchhiked to the place of his birth—to die. A good Samaritan in a Buick picked him up.

"I see that you're a drinking man," the driver said. "How far are you going?"

"Drop me at the corner!" He was affronted. He still had his pride.

The man behind the wheel said he would oblige. If, on the other hand, his passenger would stay aboard, he would tell a tale of a man who was the biggest drunk of all. Thereupon he launched himself into the story of his life.

One hundred and fifty miles later, and seeming more like ten, the self-described biggest drunk of all found a hotel and a doctor for his passenger. Like his New Testament counterpart, he left enough money for three days' care, after which he returned, claimed his passenger, and took him back to metropolis again. There he housed, fed, clothed, and daily checked his man, who, for the first time in years, was beginning to have some thoughts of repaying another human being for a favor. Thus began the long climb up—with the help of God and a man who drove a Buick.

Joining the custodial staff of a busy railroad station, B.R. was attached to a broom. Sometimes he bent himself low over the floor he swept to avoid being recognized by former peers who had long since passed him on the ladder of success. And evenings in his room, the man who once wrote poetry was learning how to spell again. It was a profitable exercise and good therapy. He joined that organization nationally identified by the letters AA and mailed a card to a few friends—the first in an annual series of thirteen, of which I still had the sixth and seventh, found in a forgotten file.

Providence smiled and contrived a happy circumstance, resulting in improved employment. Yet fate also threw a curve. His new occupation could easily require, on occasion, the social drink. Indeed, a crisis developed soon enough.

The office was losing its largest account. It was his assignment to dissuade the client from awarding it to a competitor. The customer was a profane, hard-drinking man. While meeting him for lunch, two drinks appeared as if from nowhere.

"On me."

"Thank you, no."

"Whatsamatter? You don't look like the kind that spits in it."

B.R. explained his situation simply, quietly. He didn't mind someone else having a drink. But as for himself, if he took one, he would take a hundred more. The Lord was with him. He stayed on his wagon. And the contract was renewed.

❧   ❧   ❧

One day after church, B.R. gave me a sealed envelope to be opened on the day he died. That day came in the fourteenth year of his sobriety. Unfolding the paper, I found a twofold request. He asked me to officiate at his funeral in the city of his birth. He also asked me to keep telling his story for the encouragement of those trying to get off the sauce.

That's why I am telling it now.

It was the opening sentence, however, that I have remembered word for word.

"Today a forgiven sinner has gone to heaven. What hath God wrought!"

WHAT'S THE WORLD COMING TO?!

Let me pay tribute to all those who, having reached threescore years and ten, still have a sparkle in their eyes. This seems a real accomplishment to me. It isn't easy to remain on the growing edge of life. The Bible tells us that the eye of Moses was not dim nor his natural force abated at the age of one hundred and twenty years. Remarkable! What is more exceptional, however, is not physical but spiritual youthfulness and zest when the shadows lengthen.

Many people in their forties, and even younger, are already well on their way to a crotchety old age. They are nurturing attitudes and opinions that will not result in their growing older gracefully. These are the people who compare the past to the present, always to the glory of the past. To them, the world that was is always better than the world that is. Here are some of their characteristic expressions: "Children were more obedient thirty years ago." "The church was less worldly when I was a boy." And, of course, that old stand-by, "What is the world coming to!"

These expressions are not new, as the following quotation illustrates: "Our youth love luxury. They have bad manners, contempt for authority, disrespect for their elders. Children nowadays are tyrants. They control our economy. They contradict their parents and tyrannize their teachers." These words were written

in the fifth century before Christ by the Greek philosopher Socrates. Had he persisted in this temper and
declined the hemlock, he would probably have become
as negative in his old age as his wife, Xanthippe, was
all her days. For a "What's the world coming to!"
posture, though seemingly spiritual, always produces
grandpas and grandmas whose facial lines have fallen
into unpleasant places.

This is not to suggest that we go through life blindly,
blandly. God forbids it. The Book He has written stares
sin in the face. "Look what the world has come to!"
cries the Bible in the book of Genesis, as it tells us
about the fall of man. "Look at what the world is
coming to, more and more each day!" it shouts in
Romans 1, a page as current as the daily paper. "Look
what it will yet come to!" says Paul to Timothy when
he explains that perilous times will come in the last
days. So, crepe-hangers can find much support in the
pages of God's Book. And they are right. What the
world is coming to is enough to make the angels weep.

Still, this is not where the gospel bears down with
its fullest weight. It is in this connection that two of
my favorite people come to mind. Simeon and Anna.
Both had seen enough and had lived long enough to
become sour and pessimistic. Yet both still had eyes
that sparkled—and that because neither had built an
outlook on the negative bromide, "What's the world
coming to!" It was all brought into clear focus in the
temple of Jerusalem. There these two revealed the secret of their radiant wrinkles. They had been forward-
lookers, not backward-gazers. Their theme song had
not been, "What's the world coming to!" but, "Look
at what's coming to the world!" Thus, in the temple,
holding the baby Jesus in their arms, they felt tri-
umphant—also over those few of their remaining contemporaries who had always sung their songs in minor
key.

Protestants do not have a roster of saints in the manner of Roman Catholics. But if ever they should go in that direction and build an official list, my nominees will be these two old people.

When in the pulpit I decry the times, I am being biblical. But I am being even more so when I proclaim to my congregation, in major key and with lilting voice, "Behold what has come—and who has come—to the world—and is coming again!"

WHO ARE YOUR HEROES?

Tom Mix, Charlie Gehringer, Michiel Adriaensz deRuyter. These were my boyhood idols.

Mix was a cowboy, Gehringer a baseball player, while deRuyter was a Dutch admiral of years gone by. I had heard much about him from my enthusiastic father. For a time I fully planned to merge all three of these careers into one life. My own.

All of which brings up the significant subject of our influential heroes and who they are. Mine were taken from the worlds of entertainment, sports, and naval battles. Some children of years ago found theirs in Fox's *Book of Martyrs*, an altogether better choice, I think. Where do we find ours today?

It is always interesting to see who makes the cover of *Time* magazine. It is one way to assess the temperature of the times. Not so long ago the likeness of a comedian-writer-movie producer appeared, complete with feature article. The man, undeniably, has talent. He can render sex unbelievably dirty, and religion banal. Because he is a million laughs, we have conferred on him more than a million bucks. He is definitely one of the heroes of today.

The more's the pity!

Of all the questions that come to mind in this whole area, there is one that intrigues me most. Do our heroes produce the times in which they live, or is it the reverse? These alternatives are not either-or. Nevertheless, there is something to be said both ways.

People reflect their culture. It is the age that produces the man. In a time of great political controversy, statesmen may emerge. Wars spawn generals. DeSoto, Ponce de Leon, Sir Walter Raleigh, and others are just a few of the explorers who were created by an expansionist world that had discovered itself to be round. Frontiers give birth to pioneers.

Different ages crystallize different capacities. The decades and centuries vary. One period produces the architect as the man of the century, another, the philosopher or the man of letters. There was a time, although certainly not this present one, that elevated preachers as heroes. The word "parson" (the person!) stirs the memory of a page in history when a man of my profession was a VIP.

David was essentially a poet and musician, a man of finer sensibilities. No wonder he wanted to build that temple. But the times into which he had been issued forced him to exchange, to a great extent, his quill for a sword and his harp for a spear. It was not fitting, therefore, that he should be the one to lift the house of God tall against the sky. The popular songs of the day did not extol his poetic virtues, but, rather, the fact that he had slain his tens of thousands.

As with David, so with others. West Point does not produce hero generals. Nor does the crib. Only battles do.

If the times, then, fashion their heroes, who are ours? Our sensate culture, as Sorokin labeled it, produces sensate saints, as the recent cover of *Time* suggests. A former president stated that the business of America was business. Small wonder, then, that when one of his successors appointed a poet, Archibald Mac-Leish, to a government post, the country raised its eyebrows. Ours is a materialistic world, measuring stature and success in terms of dollars and, thereby, establishing an insane set of values by which our entertainers can make more in a year than most of our school teachers earn in a lifetime. Many who are active in the humanities are kept on half-rations while we turn our pugilists into minor millionaires. Praise Ali, all creatures here below.

❉   ❉   ❉

There is another kind of hero. Those who reflect their times are good or bad, depending on what it is they reflect. The other type, however, seeks to place its mark on the age rather than the other way around. They paddle their canoes against the evil stream. They want to shape the times instead of having the times shape them.

I think young Solomon was of their stripe. As a normal boy, I am sure he worshiped not only the military heroes of his day, but also dreamed of his future in similar glorious terms. But through wisdom, divinely conferred, he sought to shift history's gears and the country's emphasis from the Secretary of War to the Secretary of State. David, though he influenced his day for good, also reflected it. Providence allowed his son to change the public mood from one that went chasing after Philistines at the drop of a helmet to one that would exchange a sword for a hammer and a saw.

Such are the heroes we must choose today. There is some evidence that there are those among us who are doing this. There are some among the younger generation who are too easily dismissed as anti-establishment when, in fact, they are only refusing to follow the accepted pied pipers of a sick generation. God has no heroes, for there are none above Him. But if He had, I am sure they would be the ones who, by His light, have found their way to Mt. Calvary and Mt. Sinai—who spend their lives for service to God and their neighbor.

WIMPY

You can stop reading right here. The following contains nothing. All of which makes me rather sad.

It could have been so different. This might have been one of the best articles I ever wrote and among the best you have ever read. You see, sometime ago I had a great idea. It came to me suddenly—as great ideas so often do. It was something of an inspiration. But, not willing then to take the time to write it all down, I merely wrote a key word in my notebook which would remind me later.

Recently I looked up my note to me. I have it before me now. It simply says, in hasty scrawl—"Wimpy."

Who or what is Wimpy? Frankly, I haven't the foggiest notion. Underneath there appears an afterthought. "Tie in with Nevada governor," it says. But what in the world is the meaning here? I have tried to dredge up whatever it was I had in mind. Yet all to no avail. The only recollection I have at this moment is that I had a stupendous idea, which, alas, is now gone forevermore—lost to posterity, lost to the world.

Seriously, I doubt that the above incident represents any considerable tragedy or loss. Still, I can't help but wonder how impoverished the world of art, literature, or even world history is because so many thoughts or ideas are forgotten or mislaid.

Perhaps we can all learn a lesson, for there is, of

course, a moral to the story. If you have a thought, hatch an idea, or generate an impulse to create something or help somebody—don't put it off. Do the whole thing now. It will make life richer for you and everybody, including your heavenly Father.

Bert Juggelaar

I read this book, thanks Nellie

Very good.